SECOND CHANCE ECONOMICS

HOW HIRING THE FORMERLY INCARCERATED
CAN UNLOCK $1 TRILLION IN GDP

First published in 2026 by Second Chance Publishing.

www.secondchancepublishing.org

Library of Congress Control Number (LCCN): 2026906895

ISBN (paperback): 978-1-971863-00-9
ISBN (hardcover) : 978-1-971863-01-6
ISBN (ebook): 978-1-971863-02-3

For my family, whose support saved my life.

*

For my friends, who lifted me up in my darkest hour.

*

For my daughters, who gave me the reason to live.

CONTENTS

PREFACE

"There is nothing like success
to blind one to the possibility of failure."
—Roger Lowenstein, American author, *When Genius Failed*

At 37, I had everything. I was the chief financial officer (CFO) of Fabric, a billion-dollar technology company where I helped scale operations, raised funding from top-tier investors, and navigated a meteoric rise in valuation. Simultaneously, I ran my own hedge fund, Chrono Capital, delivering outsized returns for my investors. I owned a home in an affluent Seattle neighborhood, had a beautiful wife, and was awaiting the birth of my second daughter. By every conventional measure, I was living the American dream. But I had an insatiable desire to work harder and achieve more. That ambition would be my downfall. In a matter of weeks, I lost it all.

As CFO of Fabric, I helped orchestrate one of the most aggressive growth cycles in the post Covid-19 pandemic boom. In just twelve months, we grew from a 50-person startup into a 350-employee company, secured $240 million from elite Silicon Valley investors, and our valuation skyrocketed from $200 million to $1.5 billion—a surge that placed us among the fastest-growing Subscription as a Service (SaaS) technology companies in the country.

At the same time, my hedge fund, Chrono Capital, was outperforming the market. Comprised of my life savings and capital from family, friends, and mentors, the fund delivered a gross return of +153% over three years—beating the S&P 500's +72%. I was riding a wave of success—until I mistook momentum and good fortune for invincibility.

By the summer of 2021, my casual curiosity about cryptocurrencies became an all-consuming passion—I fell deep down the rabbit hole. My conviction only grew stronger through conversations with a close friend who was a leading crypto expert at one of the world's largest digital asset exchanges. As he walked me through his framework for evaluating early-stage blockchain projects, I realized our skills formed the perfect hedge fund foundation: his technical expertise in protocol design paired with my traditional hedge fund experience. With our complimentary backgrounds and skill sets, we decided to launch a crypto focused hedge fund, CrossCoin Capital.

By the fall of 2021, despite macroeconomic data showing no signs of inflation, I was convinced the unprecedented liquidity injected into the system over the previous two years made inflation inevitable. I predicted that impending inflationary pressures would cause the Federal Reserve to rapidly raise interest rates resulting in a decline for growth stocks and bonds. Every asset would lose value against what I anticipated would be a prolonged period of monetary tightening and market volatility—even cash loses value in an inflationary environment.

The solution emerged from my research: decentralized finance (DeFi). DeFi refers to a blockchain-based financial ecosystem that replicates traditional financial services through peer-to-peer transactions, eliminating the need for centralized intermediaries. These smart contracts mirror conventional banking functionality but with fundamentally different operational mechanics. In traditional banking, financial institutions accept deposits and extend loans, capturing the spread between these rates as revenue while providing interest back to depositors. DeFi protocols automate this process and track it through the blockchain: crypto asset holders can supply liquidity to decentralized lending pools, earning yield generated from borrowers' interest payments. The more I learned, the more convinced I became that decentralized finance represented the most significant financial innovation of our generation.

At the time, platforms like BlockFi, Celsius and Gemini were offering retail investors between 5%-20% returns on crypto deposits. However, institutional capital remained sidelined due to accounting limitations. DeFi protocols lacked role-based access control, standardized financial reporting, and verifiable audit trails rendering these yields uninvestable for companies and investment funds. Sensing an opportunity to bridge this institutional adoption gap, I started another company, HighTower Treasury. HighTower solved the pain points for institutions by offering compliance features and professional grade financial reporting while giving these institutions access to the 5%-30% yields available in decentralized markets. I was now managing four separate companies—Fabric, Chrono Capital, CrossCoin Capital, and HighTower Treasury—simultaneously.

Through comprehensive due diligence on various decentralized finance protocols, I concluded that the Terra Luna network represented the most credible and viable platform within the DeFi ecosystem. Founded by Stanford-educated entrepreneur Do Kwon, the protocol achieved significant scale, reaching a market capitalization of approximately $60 billion. Terra's credibility was further evidenced by strategic partnerships with major e-commerce platforms and an official sponsorship agreement with Major League Baseball's Washington Nationals to accept Terra Luna's stablecoin, UST, as a form of payment in the stadium.

A stablecoin is a cryptocurrency pegged to the U.S. Dollar or gold to minimize price volatility. There were several stablecoins in circulation but Terra Luna's value proposition centered on its algorithmic stablecoin, UST, which offered investors the ability to maintain dollar parity while earning interest—eliminating both price volatility and risk of principal. The combination of Terra Luna's $60 billion ecosystem, prestigious partnerships, and stablecoin yield mechanics convinced me it represented a breakthrough in financial technology, a rare convergence of blockchain innovation and real-world utility.

In early 2022, Fabric reached a critical juncture. Despite closing a $140 million series C led by SoftBank, our growth metrics were plateauing and customer satisfaction with our product was declining. My relationship with the Board had become strained over strategic differences, and following my one-year vesting milestone in March 2022, the CEO and I discussed my transitional departure to occur sometime in the summer after my upcoming paternity leave. But no date was set for my departure, and my duties as CFO would remain the same. During this period, PayPal expressed interest in acquiring Fabric at a $1.2 billion valuation. As CFO, I vigorously advocated for the deal, recognizing it as an optimal exit amid our operational challenges, but the CEO declined, holding out for a larger exit.

Given Fabric's chaotic growth over the past year, the company was in a paradox: although we had over $230 million of cash on the balance sheet, the board of directors mandated a 25% budget reduction while the CEO secretly pushed to hire engineers in South Asia in order to complete the product capabilities that we had contractually promised customers. It was against this backdrop of competing priorities that I invested $35 million, or 15% of our corporate cash balance, into Terra Luna's stablecoin yield products through HighTower Treasury—in what appeared at the time to be a safe, secure way to generate enough interest income to hire the engineers we needed.

Simultaneously, I made a parallel strategic shift at Chrono Capital. Convinced that traditional inflation hedges were inadequate, I reallocated 75% of the fund's assets from growth equities and long-duration treasuries into Terra Luna's yield-bearing instruments through HighTower Treasury. This dual deployment of corporate and personal assets into the same protocol reflected my conviction in its safety and stability.

What began as a calculated investment strategy became a catastrophic failure—an overconcentration in an asset that I had mistakenly deemed safe and secure. Blinded at the time by ego and overconfidence, both my company's capital and my hedge fund's assets were now inextricably tied to the same investment, leaving my professional reputation and personal wealth vulnerable to a single point of failure.

In May 2022, just six weeks after making the investment, Terra Luna collapsed, erasing approximately $60 billion of market capitalization in a matter of days. Words cannot capture the depth of my despair. Darkness enveloped me. Terra Luna's collapse left me emotionally and psychologically traumatized—not simply from the destruction of my own life savings, but from the crushing realization that I had failed those who placed their faith in me—my family, my friends, my mentors, and my company. The impact was immediate and devastating. My company, Fabric, fired me. My life savings were eviscerated. My career and identity were shattered. My family was ripped apart. My life was in ruin. I thought suicide was the only logical solution.

However, amid the wreckage, I discovered an unexpected grace of unwavering support of those who believed in me beyond my failure. The support I received pulled me from the deepest recess of my own darkness. My parents became my lifeline, their unconditional love a counterweight to my self-doubt. Friends and mentors extended both emotional shelter and practical guidance, refusing to let me define myself by catastrophe.

This support network helped me stand up. Within months, I secured a position as CFO for a billion-dollar family office, marking the first step in reconstructing my professional identity. I knew at the time the road ahead would be long, but as I emerged from the darkness, I could glimpse a path forward.

Then, at 6 a.m. on a morning in October 2022—six months after the Terra collapse—my world was upended again. *Fourteen* FBI agents and four local police officers descended at my door, semi-automatic weapons and pistols drawn, their tactical gear transforming a quiet suburban cul-de-sac into a scene from a crime drama. The agents confiscated my laptop and attempted to take my phone. I immediately contacted my corporate attorney, who referred me to a criminal defense attorney.

Days later, after reviewing the warrant and government filings, my new defense lawyer called. "Nevin," he said, his voice tinged with professional disbelief, "they're alleging wire fraud. The government is saying that you didn't tell the board of directors about your investment and that omission rises to wire fraud." Confusion swept over me—I had operated within my authority as CFO, following established treasury policies, and properly recorded the investment on our balance sheet. "What?" I respond confusingly. "That doesn't make any sense. I managed all financial decisions at Fabric and I was not required to get board approval. Not only that, there was no requirement that I notify the Board about the investments I chose. Additionally, we just implemented an investment policy at the company, and this investment falls within the policy."

"OK. Send me all the material so I can review it. We'll try to get a meeting with the prosecutors," my lawyer responds.

Federal prosecutors agreed to hear our position, scheduling a meeting for January 2023. Over the following months, I worked diligently with my lawyer to create a detailed PowerPoint clearly outlining the investment's strategic rationale, my full authority as Fabric's CFO to execute such transactions, and the investment's compliance with the company's policies.

I was not present at the meeting with the prosecutors, so my attorney called as soon as it concluded. "Well, Nevin, it went as well as we could have hoped for. At the end of the presentation, the prosecutor said, 'That was an impressive presentation. You've convinced us that if we have a criticism, it's narrow. If we decide to do something, we will let you know.' We have given them a lot to think about, so let's give them time to digest all the information."

"Understood," I replied, feeling a wave of relief. *The prosecutors now know the truth and will dismiss it* I thought to myself. The prosecutors finally had the full story—surely, they would recognize this for what it was—an investment gone terribly wrong, not criminal fraud. Yet even with this cautious optimism, I wanted more certainty. I consulted eight additional white collar legal defense firms. Their unanimous assessment brought measured comfort: "there does not appear to be criminal intent," each concluded, with every law firm offering to step in and serve as counsel if charges materialized.

Bolstered by these opinions, I threw myself back into rebuilding—both professionally, through my CFO role at the family office, and personally, by working to make amends with those impacted by the losses. Every day became an exercise in balancing legal uncertainty with the pressing need to move forward.

Four months later, in May 2023, I received a call from my lawyer just after lunch. I worked in an open office layout, so I quickly moved from my desk to the nearest conference room, the glass door clicking shut behind me.

"Nevin," he said, his voice uncharacteristically tense, "I just got off the phone with the prosecutor. They're filing charges. The indictment will be unsealed within the hour, and the press release will follow shortly thereafter."

All the air left my lungs like a physical blow. I kneeled over bracing myself against the conference room table, "What?" I said meekly in shock and disbelief. "I thought they were going to let us know. Wait. What do you mean by press release?"

"I'm sorry," he interjected. "With sums of money this large, it's standard DOJ protocol. They want maximum visibility."

The moment the call ended with my attorney, I began notifying key contacts—colleagues, mentors, and most crucially, the principal of the family office where I worked. He was traveling in Morocco when my urgent message reached him. At 10 p.m. Casablanca time, my phone rang.

"Nevin," he said, his voice calm but concerned, "I got your message. Is everything ok?" I explained the situation. He responded empathetically and confidently, "oh my gosh, Nevin.

Don't worry. I am here to support you. Anything you need." *Phew* I thought. As long as I had my job, I could support my daughters and fund my legal expenses.

An hour later, the Department of Justice issued its press release alongside the indictment—a carefully crafted narrative alleging I had been terminated from Fabric and then secretly transferred company funds to enrich myself. *WHAT?!* I called my lawyer angry. "This press release is not even true! I was never terminated from my job. And the investment was not secret. The accounting team knew about the investment and it was booked on our balance sheet. I never embezzled the money—it never touched my account, and I never profited from the investment. How can the government say this?"

My attorney only offered weary resignation. "I know Nevin. We will just have to respond in court." But the damage was done. Within hours, over three hundred media outlets had picked up the story and amplified the DOJ's narrative unchallenged, their headlines cementing a false narrative.

Unfortunately, my boss, the principal of the family office, was going through a contentious divorce. Apparently, his ex-wife saw the news and weaponized the DOJ press release sending my principal a nasty email "You are a criminal, and you employ criminals; I want all the money that is owed to me!"

Shortly thereafter, I was called into the head of HR's office and told I could no longer work there. The exposure was too great. I tried to defend myself: "What happened to innocent until proven guilty?" I asked.

"I am so sorry" was the response.

I was in disbelief but ultimately grateful for the initial support he gave me, and a six-week severance.

The months that followed were a surreal experience in systemic rejection. I submitted over 100 applications for every conceivable position—from C-suite roles to entry-level finance positions—each met with either silence or rejection. My network, once robust, grew unresponsive; even close contacts only offered sympathetic shrugs.

In desperation, I applied to be a ride share driver for Uber and Lyft—rejected from both citing my pending charges. I fell further, applying to McDonalds—silence. To remain productive, I applied to volunteer positions—again, rejected citing my pending charges.

Here I stood: a master's degree, a licensed certified public accountant (CPA), a chartered financial analyst (CFA), and a proven track record as a corporate executive building businesses and managing billions—yet in the eyes of employers, I had been reduced to a headline in a DOJ press release. My qualifications, experience, and presumption of innocence had evaporated in an afternoon.

Before being ensnared in the criminal justice system, I had never knowingly met someone charged with a federal crime let alone met anyone that had been to prison. Like most Americans, I operated on the assumption that guilty pleas indicated actual guilt, and that trial convictions proved undeniable wrongdoing. My experience has erased these assumptions.

The truth is far more disturbing. Federal prosecutors wield absolute charging discretion, with minimal oversight and virtually no consequences for impropriety or overreach. The system's mechanisms, particularly the "trial penalty", create perverse incentives where going to trial to prove your innocence is cost prohibitive and risks harsher sentences than pleading guilty. Faced with sentencing differentials that can span decades—e.g. plead guilty to five years in prison or risk getting twenty years if convicted at trial—even innocent defendants routinely plead guilty to avoid the trial penalty. Compounding this injustice is the financial reality in which, depending on the complexity of the case, mounting a proper defense often requires between $500,000 to $5,000,000 in legal expenses, a sum out of reach for most.

As I began speaking with others who had been through the criminal justice system, I encountered a reality that defies society's stereotypes. The people I met—those who had pleaded guilty, those who had lost at trial, and those who had served their sentences in prison—were not the dangerous criminals popular media depicts. They were accountants and entrepreneurs, doctors and teachers, administrators and marketers. Nearly all had made a single misstep, often unintentional, that snowballed into life-altering consequences.

What shocked me most was the permanence of their punishment. Even after completing sentences and paying their debts to society, individuals faced an invisible life sentence of exclusion.

I met Ivy League graduates unemployed, and skilled tradespeople barred from licensure. Highly educated and skilled individuals were left with few options, forced out of the job market or into jobs far beneath their capabilities. Through outreach, networking, and educational programs, I have met hundreds of people working to rebuild their lives post-conviction. And nearly every time, I find myself thinking: *What a waste—this person could be doing so much more for society.* The system had not only punished them but permanently relegated them to society's periphery, squandering human potential on an unimaginable scale.

These encounters revealed a tragic paradox: the United States spends billions prosecuting and incarcerating people, then systematically prevents them from contributing meaningfully upon release—entire lifetimes of productivity and purpose, lost to bureaucratic indifference.

Although the subtitle of this book only references formerly incarcerated individuals, we must recognize the pervasiveness of those affected by the criminal justice system and the size of the population. It encompasses an immense and varied population—individuals who faced charges that were later dismissed, those who accepted plea deals, defendants convicted at trial, and people who served sentences in jails, prisons, on probation, or under home confinement.

Regardless of the specifics, each individual carries lasting scars of their involvement with the justice system. Whether they managed to avoid incarceration or spent years behind bars, the consequences ripple through their lives, negatively affecting their families, careers, and future opportunities in profound ways. The impact is both universal and deeply personal—where one's debt to society is never paid because interest accrues indefinitely.

Throughout this book, *Justice-Impacted Persons (JIPs)* refers to anyone who has been negatively affected by the criminal justice system—whether they were charged but never convicted, pleaded guilty, or endured incarceration. This could be a misdemeanor or a felony. For ease of reading, this will also encompass justice-impacted person, justice-impacted people and justice-impacted individuals. It acknowledges the breadth and lasting repercussions of the justice system while also serving as a poignant reflection on how these individuals have been treated.

The acronym "JIP" carries an unintentional yet ironic linguistic resonance—historically, "jipped" or "gypped" has been used to describe being cheated or swindled, and in many ways, justice-impacted people have experienced precisely that. In many cases, they have been denied constitutional due process, subjected to coercive plea deals, battered by unethical prosecution tactics, and stripped of the opportunity to fully reintegrate and rebuild their lives.

Across the country, well-intentioned organizations work to train and connect formerly incarcerated individuals with employment opportunities. Yet despite their dedication, these efforts remain fragmented, small-scale operations limited by geography and resources, often relying on appeals to charity rather than systemic solutions.

The conventional approach frames the reentry of individuals into society as a matter of moral obligation, emphasizing second chances and social responsibility. But this perspective misses a fundamental truth: meaningful work is not just about redemption—it is the most powerful deterrent against reoffending and a harbor for broader economic growth. Without stable employment, even the most determined individuals face near-insurmountable barriers to rebuild their lives and contribute to society.

What began as personal experience soon revealed itself as a pervasive crisis. It doesn't matter if you are a business executive or a politician, a Democrat or a Republican; this crisis transcends corporate sector and political ideology—it is fundamentally a strategic business advantage. As detailed throughout the book, companies across industries that have tapped into this overlooked talent pool report measurable improvements in workforce performance. With proper training and support, these employees consistently demonstrate higher productivity and lower turnover rates compared to their peers—a competitive edge that directly impacts profitability. Their lived experiences cultivate unique strengths: resilience forged through adversity, adaptability carved from challenging circumstances, and loyalty born from the second chance offered.

The economic implications extend far beyond individual balance sheets. When examined at scale, the full integration of justice-impacted people into the workforce represents one of the most significant untapped opportunities for national economic growth. The potential impact reaches into the trillions—not merely through direct employment gains, but through the cascading benefits of community revitalization and taxpayer savings. Reduced recidivism alone would unlock billions currently spent on incarceration, redirecting public funds toward productive investments.

This is not about charity. This is about recognizing an extraordinary market inefficiency. In an era of chronic labor shortages and skills gaps, justice-impacted people represent a vast, underutilized reservoir of potential. The organizations that first recognize and act on this insight will gain a formidable competitive advantage. The communities that embrace this approach will see transformative economic renewal. And the nation that fully harnesses this potential will achieve growth that conventional workforce strategies cannot match. Giving individuals a second chance is not just a moral imperative. It is an economic one—a trillion-dollar economic issue that can lift families, communities, and our country to great new heights.

Nevin Shetty

INTRODUCTION

Story of Sarah

Sarah grew up in an affluent neighborhood and was groomed for success by her family. From early childhood, Sarah was an exceptional student and athlete. In addition, she was an avid reader, participated in math competitions, and loved going to coding camp. In high school, Sarah developed an app and won a local start-up pitch competition. Her dream was to one day work in Silicon Valley for a big tech company and eventually start her own biotech company specializing in cancer research.

During her senior year of high school, Sarah achieved her dream—she was accepted into an Ivy League university. All her hard work had finally paid off. But the summer before heading to college, her life took an abrupt turn. She attended a large house party with her boyfriend and eventually the police were called to break it up. During the chaos, Sarah was arrested for possessing a small amount of cocaine.

Despite her parents' desperate efforts and the high-priced attorney they hired, the prosecutor refused to back down. Determined to send a message, the prosecutor insisted that no one—regardless of wealth or skin color—was above the law.

Sarah was charged with a misdemeanor—possession of a Schedule II narcotic—and ultimately pleaded guilty. There was a risk she could face up to a year in prison, leaving her and her parents gripped by anxiety for months. Fortunately, the court sentenced her to just one year of probation. A wave of relief swept over Sarah and her family. Her parents hoped Sarah could brush this aside and move along with her life.

That fall, Sarah left for college, determined to avoid trouble. She steered clear of parties, kept to herself, and focused on school. After twelve months, she successfully completed her probation. Life moved forward, and she did her best to forget the trauma caused by the police, the prosecutor, and the courts.

Three years later, Sarah's senior-year resume was impressive—impeccable grades, president of the entrepreneurship club, and a data analytics internship at a cancer research institute. Recruiters from top tech firms were vying for her attention. After applying and rounds of interviews, she received full-time offers from three big tech companies. Sarah agonized over which company to choose and ultimately picked the company where she had the best cultural fit. Sarah was ecstatic.

Four weeks later, an email from HR stopped her breath: "We regret to inform you that your offer has been rescinded." Panicked, Sarah called her father, then the HR manager. "I don't understand. Can you please explain to me why my offer was rescinded?"

"The background check, which is a standard for all new hires, shows a narcotics possession charge," said the HR manager in a firm but apologetic tone, "the company has a strict policy on this. I'm sorry, Sarah."

Desperate, Sarah reached out to the recruiting manager at the other two tech companies. She was able to negotiate an offer from one of them, but she experienced the same problem a few weeks later. Once the background check came back, her offer was retracted.

Sarah was devastated, in a dark place, and cried for weeks. She had worked hard to redeem herself, but this bad decision followed her for years. Her career aspirations in tech, which had once seemed at her fingertips, now seemed impossible.

Sarah worked as a receptionist at her father's medical practice while their lawyer tried to get her record expunged. Although this would likely be just a temporary setback in her life, Sarah's parents were extremely worried about her mental health. They found a therapist to help manage Sarah's anxiety and depression.

The Ubiquity

Every day across America, millions of men and women face similar hurdles that prevent them from joining the workforce in productive and meaningful ways. One mistake, one bad decision, or even a series of poor choices that land someone in the criminal justice system will have life-long collateral consequences not only for them, but for their families as well.

Unbeknownst to most, an astounding 77 million Americans have a criminal record.[1] Of those 77 million Americans, over 20 million have a felony conviction.[2] The unintended consequence of mass incarceration means that 1 in every 3 adults in America has a criminal record. Put another way, one-fourth of the entire U.S. population is comprised of justice-impacted people (JIPs).[1] Approximately 600,000 new JIPs enter the job market each year as they are released from U.S. jails and prisons.[1] JIPs are a large, marginalized, and underutilized population.

For individuals affected by the justice system, a criminal record creates virtually insurmountable barriers to gainful employment, eliminates housing options, and even curtails opportunities for higher education. With the deck stacked against them, statistics show that within five years of release from prison, 71% of those individuals will recidivate and return to incarceration because of violations of supervised release, parole, or probation with new arrests and new convictions.[3]

While many of these individuals leaving prison pose a low risk of reoffending, they still face substantial hurdles due to their criminal record, which reduces their ability to obtain meaningful work and find stable housing. Facing hiring and housing discrimination, and with no help to overcome these hurdles, individuals can revert to old habits or make poor decisions that ultimately recycle them back into the criminal justice system. These costs—both the taxpayer costs to prosecute and incarcerate, as well as the lost income—are not only borne by individuals and their families but also have societal and macroeconomic consequences.

Given the legal barriers and social stigma, individuals with a criminal history—which in many cases is a single misdemeanor

—earn far less than an average worker. According to research from the Brennan Center, formerly incarcerated individuals earn, on average, 52% less than people with no incarceration history, while JIPs with simply a misdemeanor earn, on average, 16% less. Taken in totality, the aggregate annual earnings lost due to criminal justice system involvement is a staggering $372 billion.[4]

This lost income is first and foremost felt by individuals and their communities. But given the scale of these losses, there are macroeconomic implications as well. Taxes are not collected, and Social Security is not paid into. Meanwhile, these unemployed and underemployed individuals drain state and federal resources through government subsidies.

Hidden Hiring Costs

Whether it is a Fortune 500 company, a small business, or a technology start-up trying to scale, hiring talent is a constant problem every business faces. Survey after survey shows that *every* sector is experiencing both a shortfall in labor and a skill gap. Not only that, according to the Bureau of Labor Statistics, the average employee turnover rate is 47%, with the professional and business service industry experiencing a 63% turnover rate in 2022.[5] This labor crisis costs employers a collective $1 *trillion* dollars a year.[6]

The financial impact varies according to the employee's role within the organization but on average the cost of replacing an individual employee can range from 50% to 200% an employee's annual salary. For hourly positions, the average cost of replacing an employee is around $1,500. However, for technical roles, the cost escalates to between 100% and 150% of the employee's salary.[7] When it comes to replacing C-suite executives, the costs can soar to approximately 210% of the executive's salary. A small business earning $2 million in revenue with 10 employees at an average salary of $50,000 will experience turnover costs and lost productivity of approximately $200,000 to $450,000 annually.[8]

Empirically, every business leader has experienced the pain of hiring—losing a quality employee, quelling a loss in morale, interviewing new candidates, and creating processes to train new employees. Every part of the journey requires significant resources—both money and time. With a labor crisis at hand, it is no surprise that business leaders are searching for new labor pools to find untapped potential.

Over the past five years, there has been a gradual movement to utilize justice-impacted people. Forward-thinking executives are setting new industry standards for inclusive employment. Many of those initiatives focus on moral duty or economic benefit at the individual level. However, there is a larger economic imperative at stake. This book provides a comprehensive roadmap for integrating individuals with criminal records into the workforce, demonstrating with data and case studies of the significant financial benefits to businesses and the national economy. The cohesion of this information forms a framework and strategic approach for decision-makers in both corporate and political spheres. The compelling economic advantages of employing JIPs include reducing labor shortages, filling critical skills gaps, and enhancing corporate social responsibility (CSR) profiles. These benefits contribute to economic growth and a safer society.

Recidivism Ripple Effect

Recidivism refers to an individual's return to incarceration due to violations of supervised release or subsequent new convictions. Recidivism is the ultimate barometer to gauge the success of the criminal justice system—and the United States is failing. Approximately 44% of individuals released from prison are rearrested within the first year of release, nearly 68% are rearrested within three years, and 83% are rearrested within nine years of release.[9]

According to research from the Council of State Governments Justice Center (CSGJC), nearly 45% of prison admissions are the result of violations of supervised release, probation, or parole.[10] This means nearly half of all incarceration admissions are violations technical in nature, such as missing an appointment with a supervision officer or failing a drug test. The CSGJC estimates the direct cost of reincarcerating individuals who reoffend at over $9.3 billion annually. The broader economic cost is even larger when factoring in lost productivity, public assistance, and other social services.

Employment is crucial in reducing recidivism rates, as numerous studies demonstrate a strong correlation between stable employment and lower reoffending rates. A study by the RAND Corporation shows inmates who participate in correctional education programs, including vocational training that prepares them for employment, are 43% less likely to return to prison within three years of release than those who do not participate. Career and educational programs run by dedicated social organizations reduce recidivism by 85% with examples like the Last Mile boasting recidivism rates as low as 4.5%, and the Prison Entrepreneurship Program recidivism rate averaging a mere 7%.[11,12]

A 2013 Washington State Institute for Public Policy study analyzed 26 correctional interventions for adult offenders. It found that prison-based basic and post-secondary education programs and employment training/job assistance delivered the highest returns on investment by a significant margin—yielding 1,862% and 4,211% return on investment respectively.[13]

Providing stable employment opportunities for justice-impacted people reduces recidivism, leading to major cost savings for taxpayers. There are approximately 650,000 individuals released from prisons each year. Using government statistics, if 68% of those individuals recidivate within three years, approximately 450,000 people cycle through courts and prisons. Prioritizing employment programs that could reduce recidivism by 85% would generate $11 billion in annual federal savings. At the state level, the CSGJC reports that in 2021, 41 states spent over

$8 billion to incarcerate more than 193,000 individuals for supervision violations and revocations.[14] Billions in savings could be redirected to other critical public services, such as education, healthcare, and infrastructure development, providing broader societal benefits.

Additionally, lowering recidivism rates reduces the strain on law enforcement. With fewer repeat offenders, there are fewer arrests, investigations, and prosecutions, translating into savings for police departments, courts, the Department of Justice, and public defenders' offices. The cumulative effect of these savings enhances the efficiency of the criminal justice system and allows for the reallocation of resources to more preventive and community-focused initiatives.

From a revenue perspective, when JIPs are employed, they contribute to the economy through increased consumer spending and tax contributions. This economic activity supports local businesses, generates revenue for government programs, and stimulates economic growth.

Furthermore, stable employment alleviates pressure on social welfare programs. Employed JIPs are less likely to rely on public assistance programs like food stamps, housing subsidies, or unemployment benefits. Without employment, many JIPs lack healthcare resulting in expensive emergency room visits. One step to address the problem is to provide healthcare. A study from the Journal of Policy Analysis and Management shows that providing Medicare to released prisoners yields a return in social benefits ranging between 350% and 1062%.[15] However, that does not address the underlying root causes.

Employing justice-impacted individuals delivers powerful economic benefits across society. Creating pathways to meaningful employment unlocks untapped potential in the workforce while eliminating the economic drag of underutilized talent. As more people secure stable living-wage jobs, their increased purchasing power stimulates consumer demand—creating a virtuous cycle of economic growth. The direct fiscal advantages are equally significant. As participation in the workforce rises, recidivism drops and reliance on public assistance declines—producing measurable savings for both the government and taxpayers.

CHAPTER 1

THE LABOR AND SKILLS GAP

"Every job looks easy when you're the not the one doing it."
—Jeff Immelt, former CEO of General Electric Company.

Imagine a country with millions of job openings, billions in lost productivity, and entire industries begging for workers—while nearly 80 million capable adults remain underemployed or locked out of the workforce. This is not a theoretical exercise; it is America today.

The United States is facing one of the most baffling labor paradoxes of our time. Restaurants cannot find cooks while formerly incarcerated chefs sit unemployed. Hospitals desperately need orderlies while people with records beg for a job with stable employment. Tech companies scramble for software engineers while prison coding programs produce top talent that no one will hire.

Yet the real scandal is not the shortage, it is the solution staring us in the face. While politicians debate immigration and executives complain about "nobody wanting to work anymore," an army of desperately motivated workers stands ready. They have trained in prison workshops, earned certifications behind bars, and now face one final barrier—our willingness to see them as assets rather than liabilities.

This is not about benevolence. It is about competitive advantage. Companies like Koch Industries and JPMorgan Chase are not hiring justice-impacted workers to be nice. They are hiring JIPs because these employees show up early, stay late, and outperform their peers. In an economy where talent is the ultimate currency, the United States is leaving billions on the table by ignoring the most driven workforce that many have never considered.

The Primary Problem

In 2022, more than 50 million Americans quit their jobs, with few returning.[1] At the end of 2023, the post-pandemic labor force participation rate stood at approximately 62.5%, compared with 67.2% at the start of the 21st century.[2] The COVID-19 pandemic also led to widespread layoffs, with many workers hesitant to return due to health concerns, changes in career priorities, or the discovery of alternative employment opportunities. This has left many industries facing chronic labor shortages and skill gaps.

As of early 2024, despite many job openings, there remains a persistent shortfall in the workforce. Industries like leisure and hospitality, professional and business services, education, and health services have been hit particularly hard. These sectors, which comprise approximately 70% of the economy, have consistently exhibited high job vacancies despite attempts to attract workers through incentives like hiring bonuses and reduced qualification requirements.[3]

The challenge of labor shortages is not limited to these sectors. For example, the coal and oil industries once relied mainly on manual labor but are now more technical. Other industries, such as the healthcare sector, face unique challenges due to burn-out and high-stress levels exacerbated by the pandemic, leaving a chronic shortage of nurses and other medical professionals.[4] Regardless of secular, structural, or technological trends, *all* industries are affected by labor shortages and skills gaps.

A 2021 survey from The National Association of Business Economics (NABE) found that 47% of respondents reported a shortage of skilled workers.[5] In addition to talent shortages, respondents cite needing to adapt company culture and practices in order to engage a younger generation.

The National Association of Manufacturers reports that one of manufacturers' top concerns is "the insufficient number of skilled workers available to fill their open jobs." The report warns that "2.1 million manufacturing jobs could go unfilled by the end of the decade if current trends continue…[which] could mean the loss of up to $1 *trillion* in lost economic impact for the U.S."[6]

The economic impacts of unaddressed labor and skills gaps are profound and far-reaching. They lead to reduced competitiveness, curtailed innovation, and, worst of all, long-term stagnation. This persistent labor shortage is further exacerbated by shifting demographics, particularly the aging population, which is reshaping the composition of the workforce and placing additional strain on the economy.

Aging Demographics

Many countries worldwide, including the United States, are experiencing significant demographic changes due to aging populations. Projections by the United Nations indicate that by 2050, the number of people aged 65 or older worldwide will double, rising from 761 million to 1.6 billion, while the number of people aged 80 or older is growing even faster. To see this from another perspective, in 2021, 1 in 10 people were aged 65 or above. By 2050, this age group is projected to account for 1 in 6 people globally.[7]

These demographic shifts result in a shrinking labor force with fewer working-age individuals to support a growing elderly population, impacting economic growth, labor productivity, and social stability. The old-age dependency ratio, which compares the number of individuals older than 64 to those between 15 and 64, is set to rise dramatically. This increase indicates fewer workers available to support pensions and healthcare for the elderly, thereby intensifying the financial strain on social security systems.

Policies and programs that retrain older workers and increase female workforce participation can help mitigate the effects of an aging population but will not solve the coming shortage. With fewer young workers entering the labor force and an increasing share of the population retiring, the traditional workforce pipeline is simply not sufficient to meet the demands of a modern economy.

To sustain economic growth and prevent productivity stagnation, businesses and policymakers must look beyond conventional labor sources and tap into underutilized reservoirs of talent. This includes JIPs, people with disabilities, immigrants, and those historically excluded from stable employment opportunities. Expanding workforce participation by removing systemic barriers and offering targeted training initiatives is not just an economic necessity, it is a strategic imperative to ensure long-term stability, innovation, and competitiveness in an era of demographic transformation.

Immigration Misconception

With a shrinking workforce due to aging demographics, the need to expand labor participation has never been more urgent. Immigration has historically played a vital role in replenishing the labor force and driving economic growth, yet misconceptions and policy barriers often prevent the U.S. from fully leveraging this demographic labor pool.

Today, many people think of immigrants as uneducated individuals crossing the border illegally. But in reality, legal immigration is an economic engine that has powered the U.S. economy since its founding 250 years ago. According to the CATO Institute, immigrants are 80% more likely to start businesses than the U.S.-born population. Although immigrants represent only 13% of the population, 35% of new businesses have at least one immigrant founder.[8]

Forty-five percent of Fortune 500 companies were founded by immigrants or their children. In 2020 alone, those companies generated $6.2 trillion in revenue and employed 13.9 million people. That revenue exceeded the GDP of Japan, Germany, and the United Kingdom, highlighting the crucial role of immigrants in job creation.[9]

Immigration is essential in filling critical labor gaps, driving economic growth, and alleviating the pressures of an aging workforce. According to the OECD, from 2013 to 2023, immigrants accounted for 47% of the workforce increase in the United States and 70% in Europe.[10]

Despite their contributions, immigrants face challenges such as language barriers, cultural differences, and the recognition of foreign qualifications. Additionally, the structure of immigration policies significantly influences the ability of immigrants to thrive in the labor market. Restrictive work visa policies and bureaucratic processes can limit mobility and employment opportunities for skilled immigrants, affecting sectors that rely on specialized knowledge and skills. Anti-immigrant legislation and sentiment drive away the top end of the immigration pool, stifle the bottom end, and further exacerbate the labor shortage and skills gap.

To address labor shortages effectively, the U.S. could dismantle barriers that prevent immigrants from fully contributing to the workforce. While immigration reform is one piece of the puzzle, another lies in tapping JIPs. By creating pathways for this marginalized group to reenter the workforce and contribute meaningfully, we can reduce the reliance on immigration, strengthen the economy, and foster a more productive labor market.

Costs of Labor Shortages

The Society for Human Resource Management (SHRM) reports that, on average, hiring a single employee costs approximately $4,129 and can take up to 42 days to fill a position.[11] These costs escalate in sectors requiring specialized skills, such as healthcare and technology, because of intense competition for talent and the intensive training required. Frequent turnovers and prolonged vacancies further inflate operational costs, negatively impacting the financial health of organizations. Deloitte Insights estimates that by 2028, manufacturers could lose up to $454 billion in production annually due to these shortages.[12] The scarcity of skilled machine operators and technicians means that companies cannot fully utilize advanced manufacturing technologies, leading to underproduction, delayed orders, and ultimately lost revenue.

A report by Korn Ferry warns that by 2030, more than 85 million jobs worldwide could remain unfilled due to a lack of skilled personnel.[13] This shortage significantly affects companies that rely on continual innovation, particularly in fields like artificial intelligence, machine learning, and data science. The inability to find experts in these areas can slow innovation cycles, impede long-term growth, and diminish a company's competitive edge in the global market. In sectors facing acute skills shortages, the competition for skilled workers leads to wage inflation, disrupting the overall salary structure and contributes to broader economic inflation. This situation often drives industries to accelerate outsourcing or automation, which can lead to job losses in other sectors with broader socioeconomic impacts.

The mounting cost of labor shortages underscores the urgent need for businesses to rethink their approach to talent acquisition and workforce development. With hiring costs rising and critical positions remaining unfilled for extended periods, companies must look beyond traditional recruitment pipelines to sustain growth and competitiveness.

Exacerbating Income Inequality

The labor and skills gaps not only affect corporate profits and national GDP but also exacerbate income inequality. It is simple supply and demand. The shortage of skilled workers allows the remaining skilled workers to command higher salaries, widening the income disparity with less skilled workers. Additionally, companies facing labor shortages accelerate automation, which, while creating opportunities in some sectors, will lead to job losses in others, affecting the broader employment landscape.

The global unemployment rate for individuals under the age of 25 is three times higher than that of adults, particularly in regions with acute skills mismatches.[14] This disparity leads to high youth unemployment, fostering social disenfranchisement, propensity to engage in criminal activity, reduced lifetime earnings, and delayed life milestones such as starting a family or home ownership. Moreover, long-term unemployment can cause skill atrophy and lead to mental health issues, further complicating job prospects and perpetuating unemployment cycles.

The Federal Reserve Bank reports that wage polarization is intensifying, with wages for high-skilled workers increasing while those for low-skilled workers in stagnation or decline. The Fed attributes technological change and globalization as the two primary forces behind job polarization.[15] Middle-class families facing an erosion in their standard of living, generally reduce consumer spending thereby creating an unnecessary headwind for economic growth. This growing wage gap exacerbates social inequality with the potential to destabilize overall economic health.

Economic insecurity, in particular concerns over job security, may also catalyze populist political movements. These movements not only deepen divisions within communities but also dampen economic prosperity. The International Labour Organization's "World of Work" report notes that more than half of 106 countries surveyed face a growing risk of social unrest due to high unemployment and rising inequality.[16] The stress induced by financial instability can also lead to adverse health outcomes, increase crime, and strain family and community structures, further eroding the economy.

Cultivating New Talent

Some of the current labor shortages can be attributed to long-term trends like automation and globalization. The first reduces demand for certain types of labor, while the second shifts jobs to different regions. With declining birth rates and efforts to stanch immigration, there are limited other traditional labor pools for business. This chronic shortage of workers is leading many companies to embrace more inclusive hiring policies, such as tapping into the massive, overlooked labor pool of individuals with criminal records. The results have been surprising.

Empirical evidence shows that if JIPs are trained and integrated into companies, they perform better than typical workers. As that evidence percolates up to corporate executives, sentiment around hiring individuals with a criminal record is shifting. In 2021, JPMorgan Chase CEO Jamie Dimon and Eaton CEO Craig Arnold co-founded and created the Second chance Business Coalition (SCBC).

The SCBC started with 29 companies signing on to promote the benefits of second chance hiring. In just a few years, that number has risen to over 50 companies joining SCBC representing over $1 trillion in market capitalization, including big names such as Microsoft, Target, Walmart, McDonald's, and PepsiCo. SCBC declares: "In a hyper competitive economy, where companies struggle to identify strong candidates at all levels of their operations, too many employers are missing out on talent within this huge segment of the U.S. population. By tapping into this pool [of JIPs], companies can access a significant number of qualified applicants who may otherwise be overlooked due to their criminal history alone."

SCBC corroborates research showing that employees with criminal records "have lower turnover and stronger loyalty to their employers." On all three major fronts—worker shortages, skills gaps, and turnover, the approximately 77 million-strong demographics of JIPs has been an overlooked talent pool.[17]

A skeptic may discount the SCBC as a progressive movement. However, the Manufacturing Institute has partnered with Stand Together and the Charles Koch Institute to promote second chance hiring. Not only does it make good business sense to create strategies and processes to tap this large labor pool, but public sentiment on the topic has evolved, given its pervasiveness. Polling indicates:

- 80% of Americans support expanding Second chance Hiring Practices[18]
- 85% of HR professionals believe that workers with criminal records perform their jobs as well or better [than their peers][18]
- 64% of millennials will not take a job without a connection to Corporate Social Responsibility[18]
- 91% of millennials said they would switch to a brand with a cause.[18]

It's no wonder that broad-based support for hiring justice-impacted people is growing—mass incarceration has touched virtually every family. In 2018, the Equal Justice Initiative reported that 113 million American adults have an immediate family member who is formerly or currently incarcerated.[19] Another survey by FWD.us illustrates the effects of mass incarceration on families:

- 1 in 7 adults has had an immediate family member incarcerated for more than one year.[20]
- 1 in 34 has had a loved one incarcerated for 10 years or more.[20]
- 1 in 4 American adults has had a sibling incarcerated.[20]
- 1 in 5 has had a parent sent to jail or prison.
- 1 in 8 has had a child incarcerated.[20]
- As a result, nearly 50% all people living in the United States have experienced incarceration in their families.[20]

Given that half of all adults in the U.S. have a family member ensnared in the criminal justice system, it is unsurprising that Americans are supportive of expanded job opportunities for people with past convictions.

CHAPTER 2

UNDERSTANDING JUSTICE IMPACTED PEOPLE

"If the only tool you have is a hammer,
it is tempting to treat everything as a nail."
—Abraham Maslow, American psychologist

Preconceived notions are hindering America's economic potential. Most assume a criminal charge equals guilt, a conviction equals just punishment—but the reality is far more complex. Our system routinely coerces pleas from the vulnerable, punishes poverty as if it were a moral failure, and ignores how unchecked prosecutorial power disadvantages Americans every single day. Yet when we move beyond these superficial judgments, we discover something remarkable: those who overcome the odds to rebuild their lives do not just inspire—they become economic powerhouses.

The formerly incarcerated who break the cycle develop unparalleled resilience, work ethic, and loyalty—precisely the qualities employers today desperately yearn for. These are not assumptions; the data proves what happens when individuals get a genuine second chance. The workers we have been taught to dismiss hold the key to unlocking a secret economic engine, if only we are able to see past the stigma to the human potential underneath.

History of Incarceration

Acknowledging the systemic issues and recognizing the historical context of incarceration helps dismantle the misconception that justice-impacted individuals are solely responsible for their circumstances. For most of recorded history, prisons served primarily as holding facilities pending trial or sentencing. The concept of imprisonment as punishment itself originated in 16th-century England and became formally institutionalized during the late 18th century in Europe and the American colonies.

During the Enlightenment era, Philosophers challenged the cruelty of corporal punishments like mutilation and public executions. In 1764, Italian philosopher Cesare Beccaria's seminal work *On Crimes and Punishments* advocated against torture and execution, arguing that punishments should be proportional to the crime. Beccaria's work established key principles for modern penal reform focused on deterrence over retribution. This intellectual shift was complemented by John Howard's 1777 exposé *The State of the Prisons in England and Wales*, which documented appalling conditions through firsthand inspections of over 200 facilities. Howard's research directly informed the 1779 British Penitentiary Act, introducing rehabilitation through structured labor and solitary confinement in sanitized institutions.

The penitentiary movement emerged from a transformative belief that prisons could rehabilitate rather than merely punish. Proponents envisioned these institutions as reformative spaces—where a convicted person might enter as a criminal and return to society as a productive citizen. This marked a radical departure from traditional punishments like public shaming, flogging, or execution, offering instead what was seen as a more humane and socially beneficial alternative. Yet despite its idealistic origins, as the penitentiary system grew it became entangled in bureaucracy and industrialization, creating complexities that have since hindered efforts at meaningful reform.

The development of modern penal systems unfolded alongside sweeping socioeconomic transformations, particularly rapid urbanization. As factories displaced agrarian economies, unsupervised working-class youth—particularly immigrant children—were systematically labeled delinquents and moral threats. Reform schools, promoted as humane alternatives to prisons, instead institutionalized racial and class biases under the guise of rehabilitation fostering a cycle of criminalization. Many who entered emerged more deeply entrenched in criminal subcultures than before their incarceration.[1]

The penitentiary never fulfilled its rehabilitative promise, instead functioning as a warehouse that amplified criminality. As early as 1825, observers documented entrenched prison subcultures—marked by coded slang, tattoos, and gang signals—that operated as survival mechanisms for both adults and youth. Inmates often turned to gang affiliation for protection, either voluntarily or through coercion. Far from curbing criminal behavior, these institutions inadvertently professionalized it, creating networks that extended beyond prison walls. This paradox revealed a fundamental flaw in the model—by concentrating offenders in violent, isolating conditions, prisons systematized the very behaviors they were designed to eliminate.

Long Reach of Slavery

Incarceration has long functioned as a mechanism of racial control. After the Civil War, while the 13th Amendment abolished slavery in 1865, its exception clause—permitting involuntary servitude as punishment for a crime—enabled Southern states to enact repressive laws known as Black Codes.[2]

The Black Codes were discriminatory laws enacted after the 13th Amendment's ratification, designed to systematically restrict African Americans' freedom and recreate slavery like economics. Modeled on pre-emancipation slave statutes, these laws deliberately curtailed Black economic mobility, political participation, and social autonomy, ensuring former enslavers maintained access to cheap, coerced labor.[3]

These codes weaponized the legal system by criminalizing mundane behaviors. Vagrancy statutes punished unemployment or homelessness, enabling mass arrests that supplied convict labor.[4] Other provisions banned loitering, nighttime movement, or alcohol possession—vague offenses that granted police unlimited discretion to target Black citizens. The codes' enforcement transformed courts and prisons into tools of racial control and economic exploitation.[5]

Upon arrest, African Americans entered a judicial system engineered to extract harsh penalties and unpayable fines. Inability to pay triggered convict leasing—a state-sanctioned system where prisoners were rented to private industries, enduring brutal conditions while generating profits for corporations and governments. This legalized forced labor created a direct pipeline from courtroom to industrial slavery.[6]

The racialized exploitation of convict leasing established patterns that evolved through Jim Crow into modern mass incarceration. The National Association of the Advancement of Colored People (NAACP) reports that today, despite comprising just 32% of the U.S. population, African Americans and Hispanics represent 56% of incarcerated people, with Black Americans imprisoned at five times the rate of whites.[7]

Understanding this historical context is essential to shifting perspectives on incarcerated individuals—recognizing mass incarceration as a form of systemic oppression as opposed to individual failure. Starting from a place of empathy and understanding allows business owners and politicians to focus on the quantitative potential of this population rather than the qualitative differences.

War on Drugs

Incarceration as a tool of racial and economic control did not end with the Black Codes or Jim Crow laws—it evolved. Decades later, the War on Drugs resurrected these mechanisms under new pretexts, using "public safety" rhetoric to justify disproportionate policing of minority communities and further entrenching systemic mass incarceration.

This modern iteration began in 1971 when President Nixon branded drug abuse as "public enemy number one," inaugurating an era of punitive drug policies. The 1973 creation of the Drug Enforcement Agency (DEA) institutionalized this approach, channeling federal resources into militarized drug enforcement while neglecting prevention or treatment programs.[8]

Despite being remembered for his small-government rhetoric, Ronald Reagan dramatically expanded federal drug enforcement, escalating the War on Drugs to unprecedented levels. His administration pioneered harsh anti-crime policies including mandatory minimum sentencing, aggressive drug laws, and funding increases for prisons and policing.[9,10] The consequences were immediate and staggering: between 1980 and 1989, America's prison population more than doubled—exploding from 315,000 to over 739,000 inmates.[11]

President Bill Clinton doubled down on punitive drug policies with the 1994 Violent Crime Control Act—the most expansive crime legislation in U.S. history. It was, and still is, the largest crime bill in the country's history. Its most notorious provision, the "three-strikes" rule, mandated life sentences for repeat offenders, including non-violent drug crimes. While marketed as targeting violent criminals, the law became a key driver of mass incarceration, flooding prisons with low-level offenders serving decades without parole.[12]

By the turn of the millennium, America's prison population had swelled to 2 million people, with approximately 25% of them serving time for drug-related offenses.[13,14] This explosion, fueled by the War on Drugs, gave the U.S. an incarceration rate four times higher than the next closest NATO Country, Great Britain. The U.S. incarceration rate is among the world's most punitive, trailing only El Salvador, Cuba, Rwanda, and Turkmenistan.[15,16]

The emphasis on punishment over rehabilitation may be good election-cycle politics but it contributes to high recidivism rates, as many individuals leave prison without the skills or support necessary to reintegrate into society, ultimately imposing an enormous financial burden on U.S. taxpayers.

Type of Offenses

While the War on Drugs significantly contributed to mass incarceration, its broader impact extended to shaping public perceptions of crime. It reinforced the idea that harsh punishments were essential for public safety. Yet the reality of incarceration is more nuanced. Most justice-impacted individuals are not violent offenders, undermining the narratives that have long justified punitive policies.

Out of the 77 million Americans with criminal records, roughly 65%—the majority—are for non-violent offenses, which include drug charges, property crimes, and misdemeanors.[17] This contradicts the widespread assumption that most people with criminal records are violent.

Even among the 20 million Americans with felony convictions, non-violent offenses are the norm. In the nation's 75 largest counties, just 25% of felony defendants face charges for violent crimes, while drug offenses account for 33% and property crimes make up 29%.[18]

That said, the distinction between violent and non-violent crimes can be misleading. The line between violent and non-violent crimes is often blurred with offenses like manufacturing methamphetamines, burglary, or even just possessing a firearm during a crime are classified as 'violent' under federal law—even when no physical harm occurs. While this does not condone or excuse the behavior, it underscores the limitations of labeling and the need for context and granular assessments when discussing criminal records and incarceration.

Federal crime data from FY 2023 reveals the most common offenses: immigration violations (30%), drug-related crimes (30%), firearms offenses (14%), and fraud (8%). The remaining 18% consists of other offenses like robbery, child pornography, and money laundering.[19] Notably, a substantial share of the incarcerated population are first-time offenders—30% had little to no prior criminal history, while only 12% were classified as career offenders.[20]

This trend aligns with global research, including a seminal Swedish study revealing that just 1% of the population was responsible for 63% of all violent crime convictions. The study identified consistent patterns among these repeat violent offenders: they were predominantly male, exhibited early-onset violent behavior, and struggled with substance abuse and personality disorders.[21]

When assessing incarcerated individuals, it is important to recognize how systemic biases distort justice. Although studies differ, the frequency of *wrongful* convictions range from 1.5% to 15.4%. Not only that, a study from the National Registry of Exonerations shows that African Americans are seven times more likely than white Americans to be *wrongly* convicted of murder.[22] These injustices, regardless of skin color, often stem from behavioral biases in investigations, prosecutorial misconduct, coerced confessions, and inadequate legal defense—systemic failures that disproportionately target marginalized communities. Acknowledging these realities is crucial for reshaping how we view justice-impacted people and the system that condemns them.

Nearly every individual entangled in the criminal justice system has made regrettable choices. These decisions range from the seemingly minor—such as associating with the wrong crowd or being in the wrong place at the wrong time—to more severe actions, like making a reckless decision under duress or unintentionally causing harm—to the more extreme—individuals who sought retribution through violence or knowingly broke the law. Yet, labelling someone a "criminal'" oversimplifies a complex and nuanced reality.

In truth, many with criminal records are first-time offenders convicted of non-violent crimes. Their stories—and the situations that shaped their paths—require a reevaluation of the stigma attached to criminal records. Only by moving beyond stereotypes can we have meaningful conversations about justice, redemption, and who deserves a second chance.

Reentering Society

While understanding offense patterns can help dispel misconceptions about justice-impacted individuals, the challenges they face persist long after their time is served. For many, reintegrating into society is fraught with systemic barriers that make successful transition nearly impossible, perpetuating cycles of recidivism and economic exclusion. There is a common belief that once an individual has served their sentence, they have "paid their debt to society" and can resume a normal life. However, this assumption ignores the lasting consequences of being touched by the justice system, which often equates to a lifelong sentence of barriers and exclusion.

Justice-impacted individuals lose more than just time—they lose vital connections with family and friends, suffer reputational damage, and often emerge financially devastated. Fines, fees, asset forfeiture, and restitution strip individuals of everything. For many individuals released from prison, their only possession is literally the clothes they are wearing. Beyond financial ruin, JIPs face legal barriers to employment, housing, and education. With social trust eroded, family bonds fractured, and the stigma of a criminal record lingering long after incarceration, the compounding disadvantages create a nearly insurmountable cycle of poverty and recidivism. Without stable income or housing, many remain trapped in the cycle rather than contributing meaningfully to society. Research reflects this grim reality—within five years of release, roughly 75% of formerly incarcerated individuals are rearrested, and within nine years individuals average five arrests.[23]

The biggest obstacle JIPs face upon reentry is employment. Over 27,000 state-level regulations restrict justice-impacted individuals from obtaining professional licenses, with each state having its own rules.[24] In Texas, JIPs are prohibited from jobs like tow truck operator, HVAC contractor, and barber. While in Illinois, a JIP is denied from working as a real estate agent, cosmetologist, and nail technician—effectively shutting them out of stable professions.[25]

Second, systemic housing discrimination actively excludes JIPs through legal barriers. Due to policies that explicitly allow discrimination, Landlords routinely deny housing applications based on criminal records—even for minor or decades-old offenses. The Prison Policy Initiative reveals the devastating consequences of this practice: JIPs face homelessness at nearly 10 times the rate of the general population.[26] Without stable housing, JIPs struggle to secure employment, maintain sobriety, or rebuild family connections, creating a nearly inescapable cycle of instability and recidivism.

Even for those determined to rebuild their lives through education, JIPs face systemic roadblocks in college admissions and accessing financial aid. A Brookings Institution study reveals that 80% of private universities and 55% of public institutions screen applicants through criminal history questions—creating an immediate barrier to enrollment before academic qualifications are even considered. Until recently, federal aid restrictions explicitly barred students with drug-related convictions, disqualifying an estimated 12% of potential college attendees.[27,28] These policies force many to abandon higher education as an unrealistic path, despite research and economic data showing that access to education can change the paradigm at both the individual and national level.

The legal and systemic barriers confronting justice-impacted individuals do not just punish—they trap. By systematically denying access to employment, housing, and education, human potential is squandered and economic productivity lost. This exclusion perpetuates recidivism and poverty, leading to staggering social costs such as higher expenditures on law enforcement, incarceration, and ultimately, welfare—Medicaid, food subsidies, tax breaks, and housing assistance.

Addressing these challenges through comprehensive policy reforms not only uplifts JIPs by providing them with the tools and opportunities necessary for successful reintegration but also strengthens the broader economy by unlocking untapped labor potential, reducing dependency on public assistance, and lowering crime rates. Ultimately, fostering successful reintegration benefits everyone—reducing taxpayer burdens, enhancing public safety, and building stronger, more resilient communities.

Socioeconomic Starting Point

For justice-impacted individuals, reintegration involves overcoming far more than just the stigma of a criminal record. Many return to the same systemic inequities that contributed to their initial involvement with the justice system: impoverished neighborhoods with scarce job opportunities, underfunded schools, and fractured community support networks. The data paints a stark picture. According to Bureau of Justice Statistics, incarcerated individuals had a median income 41% lower than their non-incarcerated peers *before* imprisonment.[29] This economic disadvantage is compounded upon release, as they return to communities often lacking basic resources and opportunities. Without intervention, this creates a self-perpetuating cycle where poverty, limited education, and neighborhood disadvantage continue to shape and recycle life outcomes long after release.

Additionally, educational disparities between incarcerated individuals and the general population reveal a troubling pattern. While just 14% of U.S. adults lack a high school diploma or equivalent, this number more than doubles to 33% among the incarcerated population—meaning individuals in prison are 2.4 times likely to lack a high school education. This glaring gap highlights how educational disadvantage often precedes and potentially contributes to incarceration.[30]

These data points illustrate a correlation between socioeconomic disadvantage and a higher likelihood of incarceration—limited education and poverty create cascading disadvantages from childhood trauma to unstable home environments. Deprived of social capital and economic mobility, marginalized individuals become trapped in a self-perpetuating cycle—where poverty increases incarceration risk, and incarceration dampens economic mobility. Breaking this cycle is crucial not only for the individuals affected but also for society writ large, as it has the potential to transform lives and stimulate prosperity for all.

Green Shoots

Despite encountering systemic barriers—both legal and societal—many JIPs have not only transformed their own lives but also made meaningful contributions across diverse professional fields. Research consistently demonstrates that JIPs who secure stable employment are far less likely to reoffend, with studies showing recidivism rates dropping by as much as 60%.[31] Moreover, JIPs who are given a second chance in the workforce often prove to be more resilient, loyal, and committed employees compared to their non-JIP peers—further underscoring their determination and the value of this labor pool.

To the surprise of many, the U.S. Army permits individuals with felony convictions to enlist but with a critical stipulation—candidates must demonstrate "sound moral character" by submitting detailed case documents, a personal narrative, and proof of rehabilitation. This selective process prioritizes self-motivated individuals who have overcome adversity, offering a scalable model for private employers to emulate. The results speak for themselves. According to the Trone Center for Justice &

Equality, enlisted personnel with felony records are 33% *more* likely to earn a promotion to sergeant than their peers without such backgrounds—proof that second chances can drive exceptional performance.[32]

In another example, at Total Wine & More, HR managers found that employees with prior records had 12.2% lower annual turnover compared to their peers. Similarly, Electronic Recyclers International (ERI)—North America's largest electronics recycling firm—launched a targeted JIP hiring initiative and slashed turnover from 25% to just 11%.[32]

Televerde, a company specializing in providing job opportunities and skills training for incarcerated women, has successfully reduced recidivism rates and empowered its participants. Operating call centers within women's correctional facilities, the company has helped over 4,000 women transition back into society, achieving a remarkable recidivism rate of under 6%—far below the national average of 58%. Graduates of Televerde's program see employment rates 91% higher than average and earn four times more than typical wages for formerly incarcerated women.[33]

Dave's Killer Bread illustrates the potential with second chance hiring as well. Approximately one third of the company's employees have criminal records—and rather than holding the company back, it strengthened the company's corporate culture and been a key part of their success. Growing from a small local operation into a national brand, in 2023 Dave's Killer Bread eclipsed $1 billion in sales.[34,35]

The evidence demonstrates that justice-impacted individuals represent a valuable and underutilized workforce resource. Across multiple industries, these employees consistently exhibit high retention rates and deliver strong performance. Their lived experiences often translate into distinct workplace advantages, including resilience, problem-solving skills, and commitment to professional growth.

This workforce potential emerges against a historical backdrop where punitive sentencing and incarceration has remained the predominant response to crime for over two centuries, despite limited evidence of its effectiveness improving public safety or as a deterrent mechanism. Contemporary research increasingly suggests that alternative approaches, particularly those emphasizing education and employment opportunities, yield superior outcomes. When individuals exiting the justice system gain access to meaningful employment, the benefits extend beyond personal transformation to include measurable economic advantages for businesses and communities alike. By empowering individuals to contribute positively to society, we create a flywheel of growth, turning what was once an economic drag into a powerful engine for prosperity.

CHAPTER 3

THE COSTS OF IGNORING JUSTICE-IMPACTED PEOPLE

"Don't fight forces; use them."
—Buckminster Fuller, American inventor & architect

Each time we prioritize prisons over classrooms, punishment over potential, we are not just locking away people—we are locking in generational decline. The data exposes the stark truth that we spend more to imprison people than educate children, more to prosecute individuals than heal communities, more to dismantle families than to build pathways to opportunity. When we sacrifice potential for retribution, we condemn the entire country to a future defined not by progress, but by perpetual decay.

This is not justice—it is economic self-sabotage on an unprecedented scale. While other nations nurture human potential, the United States pours resources into a system that strangles it. The Unites States has built an engine of harm that does not merely penalize crime—it mass produces it, robbing children of caregivers, draining workforce participation, and misallocating resources on a historic scale. Every dollar funneled into this cycle does not just maintain the status quo—it actively undermines our nation's collective capacity to thrive.

The most damning indictment is not found in prison cells, but in what we have sacrificed to fill them: small businesses never opened, engineers whose blueprints gathered dust, teachers and nurses who became inmates instead. We have confused punishment with safety. Real security comes from paychecks, not prison walls. Reform is not about leniency; it is about being smart on growth. Because a nation that builds more prisons than opportunities is not tough—it is terrified of its own potential.

Massive Misallocation of Resources

The United States continues to prioritize punishment over prevention, funneling billions of dollars into incarceration while underinvesting in education and rehabilitation. The United States spends approximately $44,000 to *simply house* an inmate at a Bureau of Prisons (BOP) facility while the average annual cost at state and county facilities is $47,000.[1,2] In juxtaposition, the United States spends on average only $17,000 annually per K-12 student.[3] That means the United States spends 2.6 times more on warehousing human beings than on educating our nation's children.

The grotesque math deepens at the state level. In 2023, the annual cost to incarcerate one person in California reached a record $133,000.[4] In contrast, the average spent annually per K-12 student in California is only $18,000.[5] California spends over 7 times more to incarcerate an individual than to educate a student.

In 2024, the Department of Justice's (DOJ) budget allocated approximately $2.9 billion directly to U.S. Attorneys' Offices.[6] According 2020 – 2022 data from the Bureau of Justice Statistics

(BJS), approximately 68,000 individuals are charged with a federal crime annually. Using separate government data, Pew Research reports that only 2% of federal defendants proceed to trial.[7] Of the approximately 68,000 people charged with a federal crime each year, a mere 1,300 go to trial, meaning that the Department of Justice spends on average $2,100,000 per trial.[8,9,10]

Critics may defend that taxpayers spending, on average, $2.1 million per trial is worth punishing bad actors and keeping criminals off the streets. However, the cost appears like gross negligence when compared to an alternative solution that results in *safer* communities and yields significant cost savings to taxpayers—pretrial diversion. As a formal alternative to traditional prosecution, pretrial diversion programs redirect defendants into community-based rehabilitation services.

While the DOJ has resisted broader implementation of pretrial diversion programs—arguing they are "inappropriate and unnecessary for the federal criminal system"—empirical evidence directly contradicts their stance. The proliferation of 56 federal diversion initiatives in the face of this opposition reflects growing recognition of their efficacy.[11]

Peer-reviewed studies and program evaluations indicate that these interventions demonstrate substantial reductions in both recidivism rates and costs compared to traditional prosecution. A 2011 study of the District of Massachusetts drug treatment pretrial diversion program showed a 37% decrease in recidivism. Similarly, a 2016 pretrial diversion study in the Central District of Illinois showed a 44% reduction in recidivism alongside $7.7

to $9.7 million in taxpayer savings. Perhaps most strikingly, the Southern District of California's Alternative to Prison Solutions (APS) program achieved a 3.2% recidivism rate, saving taxpayers $10.4 million—with a cohort of just 476 participants.[12] These outcomes are particularly notable given the modest operational cost of diversion programs which average a mere $700 to $1,600 per individual *annually*.[13] Sending just 10% of eligible offenders to community based treatment programs rather than prison would save taxpayers $4.8 billion.[14]

In fiscal year 2024, the DOJ distributed $67.3 billion among its 11 subagencies, which include the Federal Bureau of Investigation (FBI), Federal Bureau of Prisons (BOP), Drug Enforcement Administration (DEA), and Bureau of Alcohol, Tobacco, Firearms and Explosives (ATF).[15] With approximately 160,000 federal inmates in BOP custody and an additional 68,000 individuals federally prosecuted annually, the DOJ's average cost to investigate, prosecute and incarcerate is $300,000 per person.[16] In contrast to the approximately $17,000 spent annually per K-12 student, the U.S. spends 17.6 times more prosecuting an individual than educating a child.

Indirect Costs

Although the direct costs of investigating, prosecuting, and imprisoning individuals are immense, the indirect costs borne by society are more staggering. Once the criminal justice system ensnares an individual, the collateral consequences are catastrophic and far-reaching—lost earnings, financial distress, adverse health effects, strain on welfare systems, and damage to families. In an acclaimed 2016 study, *The Economic Burden of Incarceration in the U.S.*, from Washington University in St Louis, the research team found that for every dollar in incarceration costs, there is an additional $10 in social costs. The research team assigned monetary values to twenty-two different variables, including factors like moving and eviction costs, costs of increased infant mortality rates, additional burden on welfare programs, and costs of increased criminality of incarcerated progeny. When accounting for these federal and state costs, the total expense of our criminal justice system is $1.2 *trillion*.[17]

In 2023, the U.S. GDP was approximately $27.4 trillion, meaning the total cost of the criminal justice system amounts to 4.4% of GDP annually.[18] To put that in perspective:

- The average U.S. GDP growth rate since 1980 has been approximately 2.6%
- The average U.S. GDP growth rate during the boon of the 1990s was 3.2%
- The US GDP growth rate during the 2021 post-pandemic boom was 5.8%

A punitive mindset and inability to make meaningful justice reform costs the U.S. approximately $1.2 trillion or 4.4% of additional GDP growth *every single year*.

Collateral Damage (to Families)

The human cost of incarceration extends far beyond prison walls, creating trauma that reverberates through families and communities. The systemic collateral damage includes financial instability, psychological stress, and the perpetuation of cyclical poverty, creating a complex web of challenges that extend through generations. The ripple effect is becoming more pronounced given that nearly 50% of all American adults have an immediate family member who has been incarcerated.[19]

When a family member is incarcerated, the immediate financial consequences, along with the emotional and psychological toll, are severe. Incarceration often results in the loss of a primary breadwinner; resulting in an average 22% reduction in total household income, even when accounting for supplemental income sources.[20] These economic impacts are particularly acute among low-income families, who lack savings to absorb such shocks.

Research underscores the substantial economic burden that incarceration imposes on families and communities. A study by the Institute for Justice Research and Development highlights that "more than half the costs of incarceration are borne by families, children, and community members who have committed no crime".[21] These costs include legal fees, court-imposed fines, and travel expenses to visit incarcerated loved ones—financial obligations that disproportionately strain low-income households. The economic strain is severe with findings from the Ella Baker Center for Human Rights showing that 65% of families with an incarcerated member struggle to afford necessities, including food, housing, and medical care, due to these additional financial burdens.[22]

A National Institutes of Health study documents significant health consequences for families affected by incarceration, revealing that spouses and children of incarcerated individuals demonstrate substantially higher rates of anxiety, depression, and physical health complications. These adverse health outcomes compound familial stress levels, creating secondary effects that extend to reduced workplace and academic productivity.[23]

The intergenerational consequences are particularly acute for children, who face a sixfold increase in psychological disorders compared to their peers. This population also demonstrates markedly higher risks of juvenile justice system involvement, perpetuating cycles of intergenerational incarceration.[24]

Parental incarceration perpetuates cycles of poverty by imposing significant long-term economic disadvantages on affected children. The Annie E. Casey Foundation reports that approximately 5 million American children—about 1 in 15—have at some point experienced parental incarceration and are more likely to experience developmental delays and educational challenges.[25] Additionally, these children experience substantially higher poverty rates, with consequences extending well into adulthood. Studies indicate children with incarcerated parents are 48% more likely to drop out of school than their peers, severely limiting their career prospects, earning potential, and economic contribution.[26]

Incarceration erodes social capital and destabilizes community networks. A study published in the Journal of Criminal Law and Criminology found that high incarceration rates fracture interpersonal relationships, diminish trust, and weaken collective efficacy—key components of social cohesion. These breakdowns correlate with declining civic participation and elevated crime rates, creating a self-reinforcing cycle of community deterioration.

Additionally, families impacted by incarceration frequently rely on public assistance programs—including housing subsidies, supplemental nutrition assistance programs (SNAP), and Medicaid—to meet basic needs, further straining government resources. The cumulative financial burden of lost productivity, increased welfare dependence, and elevated social service expenditures represent a $1 *trillion* opportunity to overhaul the criminal justice system. Redirecting these resources toward rehabilitation and community investment could yield substantial returns— higher wages, increased tax revenues, and reduced spending on social services.

In the absence of systemic reform, nonprofit organizations have emerged as critical intermediaries, implementing family support programs and community-based reentry initiatives to mitigate the long-term damage of incarceration. Efforts such as the Justice Reinvestment Initiative have demonstrated measurable success in facilitating reintegration and reducing recidivism, underscoring the potential of community-driven solutions.[27]

A more sustainable approach would involve reallocating budgets toward these evidence-based services, which not only save taxpayers billions but improve public safety and increase economic output. However, until comprehensive policy changes are enacted, such interventions and initiatives from nonprofit organizations simply remain as essential stopgaps.

Public Health & Safety Costs

The cyclical nature of incarceration and high recidivism rates generates substantial societal burdens, manifesting in both significant financial costs and profound humanitarian consequences. Research reveals disturbing correlations between incarceration and worsening mental health crises, with the Bureau of Justice Statistics reporting that 37% of prisoners and 44% of jail inmates experience mental health disorders.[28] These untreated conditions create a dual burden: they contribute to repeated incarcerations while straining public health systems ill-equipped to provide adequate care.

Substance abuse disorders compound these challenges, serving as both a driver and consequence of criminal justice involvement. Rather than receive proper treatment, countless individuals who meet clinical criteria for substance dependence cycle through jails and prisons, exacerbating patterns of homelessness, unemployment, and recidivism. Each avoided intervention represents a lost opportunity for rehabilitation and an ongoing drain on public resources. The scale is unprecedented as approximately 65% of the U.S. prison population meets the criteria for substance use disorders.[29] The United States bears a staggering economic burden from substance abuse, with total annual costs reaching approximately $193 billion annually.[30] This includes approximately $12 billion in healthcare costs, $61 billion in criminal justice costs, and $120 billion in productivity losses.[31]

According to a 2018 report by the Council of Economic Advisers, rehabilitation programs targeting mental health and substance abuse disorders among incarcerated populations demonstrate significant economic benefits. While program effectiveness varies, these interventions consistently yield positive returns on taxpayer investment ranging from 147% to 527%.[32] Comprehensive, integrated treatment for incarcerated individuals with substance abuse and mental health disorders is critical to lowering recidivism and alleviating public health expenditures. Evidence demonstrates that targeted interventions can reduce recidivism by up to 50%, highlighting the urgent need for investment in comprehensive rehabilitation programs—not only to improve individual outcomes but also to yield long-term societal benefits.[33]

The connection between recidivism and homelessness further exacerbates public health challenges. Research shows formerly incarcerated individuals face a tenfold increased risk of homelessness compared to the general population.[34] This vulnerability leads to cascading consequences: higher transmission rates of communicable diseases, disproportionate reliance on emergency medical services, and repeated cycling through emergency rooms, shelters, and jails. Without stable housing, JIPs encounter a devasting loop that imposes enormous societal costs—both in immediate healthcare expenditures and long-term economic losses from sustained instability.

Evidence-based interventions like the Housing First model offer a proven solution to break the cycle of homelessness and incarceration. Unlike traditional housing programs that impose conditions like employment or sobriety as prerequisites, Housing First operates on a stability-first principle—providing immediate, unconditional housing alongside voluntary support services such as mental health counseling and job training. The results are striking. Cities like Houston and Salt Lake City reduced chronic homelessness by 60% within five years of adopting the model. By addressing basic human needs first, the model disrupts the homelessness-to-prison pipeline and creates a foundation for long-term recovery.

Critically, the benefits of housing stabilization extend far beyond individual outcomes. Reduced homelessness correlates with measurable decreases in public disturbances and police interventions, allowing law enforcement resources to be reallocated. Simultaneously, justice-impacted individuals gain the stability needed to enter the workforce, increasing local tax bases and stimulating consumer spending. This virtuous cycle demonstrates how evidence-based interventions like Housing First improve public health outcomes while functioning as economic development strategies, transforming social burdens into productive contributors.[35]

The profound public health consequences of recidivism—including untreated mental illness, substance use disorders, and chronic homelessness—reveal systemic failures of our current justice system. Data demonstrates how the recidivism ripple effect compounds into a public health crisis and economic burden that drains communities, healthcare systems, and public resources. These interconnected crises demand a fundamental shift in approach, one that prioritizes prevention and rehabilitation over punishment.

The Cure

Stable employment serves as one of the most effective tools for reducing recidivism, simultaneously strengthening public safety and economic growth. Research demonstrates that JIPs who secure employment are far less likely to reoffend than those who remain unemployed. A United States Sentencing Commission study found that JIPs who obtain work within their first-year post-release reduce recidivism rates by 40%.[36] Beyond individual outcomes, communities with higher JIP employment rates also see measurable declines in crime, proving that workforce reintegration is not just personal rehabilitation—it is a public safety imperative.[37]

Across the country, innovative programs are proving that economic empowerment can break the cycle of recidivism. A standout example is Texas' Prisoner Entrepreneurship Program (PEP), which equips JIPs with the tools to secure stable employment or launch a business. Since its founding in 2004, PEP has graduated over 3,500 participants from its rigorous curriculum, covering business fundamentals, leadership, and personal development. The results speak volumes as 96% of graduates find employment or start businesses within 90 days of release, and their recidivism rate is under 9%—far below the national average of 68%. Remarkably, this transformative impact comes at a cost of just $2,800 per participant, a fraction of the cost of incarceration.[38]

Defy Ventures stands out as another proven model for breaking the cycle of incarceration through education and entrepreneurship. Since its launch in 2010, the organization has expanded its Entrepreneurs in Training (EIT) program across multiple states, including California, New York, and Colorado. By 2022, Defy Ventures had empowered over 5,000 participants with outstanding results at an incredible value: over 500 businesses launched, a recidivism rate of under 8%, and a cost per graduate at a mere $2,000—demonstrating both transformative impact and fiscal efficiency.[39]

Columbia University's Justice Through Code program, established in 2020, has demonstrated remarkable success in its mission to train justice-impacted individuals as full-stack software engineers. Through its rigorous year-long curriculum, the program has graduated 300 fellows achieving a 97.5% employment rate among participants. Many graduates have secured positions with leading companies including Amazon, Oracle, Capital One and Walt Disney, with numerous individuals earning six-figure salaries.[40] Most impressively, the program's 2023 Impact Report revealed a recidivism rate of less than 1%, showcasing the transformative potential of high-quality technical education for JIPs.

These programs represent a cost-effective alternative to the substantial taxpayer burdens associated with recidivism and lost productivity. Catalyzing employment deters crime, reduces recidivism, fosters community engagement, and enhances societal well-being. Additionally, JIPs with steady employment often serve as role models for at-risk populations, demonstrating the transformative power of employment at both individual and community level.[41]

In 2015, the U.S. Department of Labor launched the Reentry Employment Opportunities (REO) program, a targeted initiative to improve employment outcomes for JIPs. By forging partnerships and implementing evidence-based strategies, REO achieved dramatic results reducing recidivism by up to 69% among participants.[42] This success underscores a fundamental truth: stable employment is the foundation of successful reentry, simultaneously lowering the societal costs and unlocking economic potential. When justice-impacted people secure meaningful work, they transition from burdens to contributors—strengthening community safety, stimulating local economies, and proving that reintegration is not just possible, but profitable.

CHAPTER 4

THE BUSINESS CASE FOR SECOND CHANCE EMPLOYMENT

*"As far as men go, it is not what they are that interests me,
but what they can become."*
—Jean-Paul Sartre, French philosopher & novelist

Corporate America is trapped in a self-inflicted talent crisis. As businesses drown in recruitment costs and churn through disengaged workers, they are systematically excluding a tenacious, loyal workforce—justice-impacted individuals hungry for opportunity. The uncomfortable truth is that our hiring biases have blinded us to an extraordinary competitive advantage.

Second chance employees do not just fill roles—they transform workplaces. Their lived experiences cultivate an unparalleled work ethic—a powerful blend of resilience, determination, and appreciation that no business school can replicate. JIPs do not just work for a paycheck; they work to prove their worth and reclaim their future.

Employers are awakening to the powerful truth that resilience and perspective forged through adversity create uniquely valuable employees. Forward-thinking companies that look beyond criminal records are making a transformative discovery: when you hire people others will not, you get performance others cannot.

The data is clear. In today's competitive labor market, businesses clinging to outdated hiring prejudices are not being cautious—they are being outmaneuvered. In the war for talent, the ultimate edge may come from those we have counted out.

Reducing Turnover, Recruitment, and Training Cost

Beyond the social and economic arguments for hiring justice-impacted individuals, there is a compelling business case backed by data: companies that embrace second chance employment report lower turnover, reduced recruitment costs, and unmatched employee loyalty, translating directly to stronger financial performance. A joint study by the Society for Human Resource Management (SHRM) and the Charles Koch Institute found that 82% of managers view second chance employees as equal or more valuable than their peers.[1] A 2023 article in the MIT Sloan Management Review affirmed that 85% of HR leaders report that second chance hires perform equal to or better than employees without criminal records.[2] The findings underscore the potential of JIPs to be valuable, long-term contributors to the workforce.

Research from the Institute for Emerging Issues highlights that employers experience lower turnover costs when hiring formerly incarcerated individuals. Specifically, the turnover rate for JIPs is anywhere from 3% to 85% percent lower depending on the sector and how the program is implemented compared to non-JIP hires, resulting in significant savings in recruitment and training expenses.[3,4] Given that replacing an employee typically costs 50–200% of their annual salary, these retention gains translate into substantial savings for organizations.[5]

Additionally, companies typically spend substantial amounts on staffing agencies to fill open positions, with placement fees ranging from 10% to 25% of a new hire's first-year salary.[6] By partnering with nonprofit organizations specializing in justice-impacted placements, employers can dramatically reduce—or even eliminate—these recruitment costs. Many NGOs offer talent placement services at minimal or at no cost to companies, generating thousands of dollars of savings per hire while connecting businesses with pre-vetted, highly motivated candidates. The dual advantage of reduced acquisition costs and quality hires makes NGO partnerships an increasingly strategic component of modern talent acquisition programs.

In addition to reducing turnover and recruitment costs, businesses can save on training expenses by hiring JIPs. Many JIPs acquire targeted vocational skills during incarceration through programs designed to align with industry needs—from manufacturing and culinary arts to software engineering. As a result, these candidates often arrive job-ready, equipped with technical competencies that minimize onboarding and allow for faster productivity. This streamlined integration not only cuts training budgets but also accelerates workforce contributions, creating a double benefit for businesses.

Utilize Tax Incentives & Grants

Various government agencies encourage the employment of JIPs through financial incentives. These programs, including tax credits and bonding initiatives, offer direct economic advantages to participating employers. A prime example is the Work Opportunity Tax Credit (WOTC), which provides up to $9,600 in federal tax credits per qualified hire from designated groups facing employment barriers, making it an attractive incentive for hiring JIPs.[7,8]

The WOTC program delivered significant economic benefits in 2022, with over 2.5 million tax credits issued to U.S. employers—totaling approximately $6 billion in savings.[9] These incentives reduce corporate tax liabilities while actively promoting workforce participation. The program's impact underscores how policy-driven financial mechanisms can effectively advance both business objectives and second chance hiring, creating measurable value for employers and communities alike.

Another valuable government incentive is the Federal Bonding Program (FBP), which provides fidelity bonds at no cost to businesses, that protect against potential losses related to employee dishonesty, fraud, or theft. This program directly mitigates the commonly perceived financial risks associated with hiring JIPs. Since its creation, the FBP has facilitated over 42,000 job placements for at-risk candidates with only 460 claims filed—demonstrating an exceptional 99% success rate.[10] By addressing the perceived financial risks of second chance hiring, the FBP serves as both an insurance policy and a strategic workforce development tool. For employers, it represents a risk-free way to access an overlooked talent pool. The program's remarkable success rate proves that concerns about hiring JIPs are largely unfounded, making the FBP one of the most effective—yet underutilized—tools in today's competitive labor market.

The economic benefits of these incentive programs are well documented. A Texas A&M University study analyzed Project RIO in which the Texas Employment Commission facilitated employment for JIPs through bonding programs and support services—the initiative saved Texas taxpayers over $10 million annually. Beyond savings, the program transformed economic trajectories as participants transitioned from relying on state assistance to becoming taxpayers themselves. These outcomes demonstrate how targeted employment initiatives create a double dividend of reducing system costs while expanding the tax base.[11]

The WOTC and FBP allow employers to access the JIP talent pool while reducing financial risk. Charles Maymon, Regional CEO of American Ambulance Service, endorses the program's value: "I have simple words for employers. Use the Federal Bonding Program…There's nothing but upside to it, and truly you're getting the most wonderful employees that are out there".[12] This testimonial underscores how the FBP transforms perceived hiring risks into tangible competitive advantages. These financial incentives deliver concrete operational advantages by reducing business costs, strengthening workforce capacity, and gaining a strategic solution to labor shortages.

Reduce The Labor Gap

Justice-impacted individuals often possess various skills and experiences that employers overlook due to stigma or misconceptions. Companies that adopt fair-chance hiring practices gain access to this high-potential talent pool, addressing critical labor shortages across all types of roles. Proven initiatives across industries show that with targeted training and opportunity, JIPs can thrive professionally to help businesses build competitive, future-ready teams.

The hospitality sector continues to face severe workforce challenges, with over 2 million unfilled positions across the industry in 2024.[13] Similarly, the restaurant industry faces a shortfall of about 400,000 workers below pre-pandemic levels.[14] Innovative programs like Chopping for Change (C4C) are proving this crisis also presents an opportunity. Based at Ohio's Northeast Reintegration Center, C4C's intensive 18-month culinary training program transitions incarcerated individuals into civilian custody while providing culinary arts training, counseling, and support services. This comprehensive and intensive program works—the recidivism rate for C4C graduates is an astounding 0%.[15]

The U.S. technology sector faces a critical workforce shortage as well, with the Bureau of Labor Statistics reporting 1.8 million software developer openings in 2022—a number projected to grow 25% over the next eight years.[16] Addressing this need, The Last Mile program pioneered an innovative solution from the San Quentin State Prison in 2010. This groundbreaking initiative provides incarcerated individuals with comprehensive software development training, creating a pipeline of job-ready tech talent. Graduates have secured employment with leading companies including Dropbox, Slack and Zoom. The Last Mile has educated over 1,400 individuals and boasts a recidivism rate of just 4.5%.[17]

The construction industry faces similar labor shortfalls reporting 1.6 million unfilled positions in 2022 with an anticipated 151,000 new job openings each year.[18] As McKinsey & Company's recent report "Will a labor crunch derail plans to upgrade US infrastructure?" underscores, industry leaders are increasingly partnering with reentry programs to address this gap. Tapping into this worker reservoir, San Bernardino County launched Prison-2-Employment, a collaboration between county agencies and the Building Industry Association that connects JIPs with entry-level opportunities at 30 local construction firms.

The National Center for Construction Education and Research (NCCER) highlights the measurable benefits of hiring JIPs, including enhanced employee retention and the reduction of critical skill shortages. These programs bridge the gap between untapped potential and workforce needs, proving that with proper training and support, JIPs can excel across industries and roles. By integrating skilled labor from non-traditional sources, companies not only resolve immediate staffing challenges but also cultivate a more stable, productive workforce—reducing turnover, strengthening operational capacity and increasing productivity.

Improve Productivity

Despite persistent stereotypes, data and employer testimonials consistently demonstrate that justice-impacted individuals bring exceptional dedication and loyalty to the workplace. While stigmas continue to deter many employers, the reality reveals that JIPs are frequently among the most motivated and reliable team members. Beyond addressing recruitment and retention challenges, hiring JIPs delivers measurable productivity gains through infusion of diverse perspectives that drive productivity, heighten overall employee morale, and increase access to a talent pool with demonstrated resilience and commitment. These benefits collectively challenge outdated assumptions while delivering tangible business value.

Integrating JIPs into the workforce yields significant benefits for team performance and organizational success. Companies like Dave's Killer Bread and Homebird Industries have documented how JIP employees frequently demonstrate exceptional commitment and lower turnover rates, directly contributing to workforce stability and productivity gains. Research from the Center for Employment Opportunities (CEO) reveals a consistent pattern where employers underestimate the likelihood of justice-impacted individuals earning a five-star rating once employed.[19]

Concrete examples demonstrate this impact: a Toyota manufacturing plant in Kentucky implemented a second chance hiring pilot program that increased workforce diversity by 8% while reducing monthly turnover by 70%.[20] Similarly, in Michigan, 25 for-profit companies fund The Source, a nonprofit designed to support second chance workers. The thesis was radical—stabilizing employee's lives would be good for our businesses—and it proved successful with companies reporting an average 330% return on their investment.[21]

Justice-impacted individuals bring resilience and distinctive perspectives to the workplace, leading to strengthened team dynamics. Their determination to prove worthy of a second chance and diverse life experiences creates a more adaptable and engaged work environment. Research underscores the tangible benefits of such experiential diversity: a Gallup study revealed that organizations with highly engaged employees—a hallmark of inclusive workplaces—achieve 21% higher profitability.[22] Furthermore, companies with diverse leadership teams are 35% more likely to financially outperform their peers, and diverse workforces generate 2.3 times more cash flow per employee than non-diverse companies.[23]

Amid ongoing labor shortages and the widespread impact of mass incarceration, recent data reveals growing acceptance of second chance employment. According to a 2021 Fair Chance Hiring Report, an overwhelming 80% of U.S. employees support their companies hiring individuals with criminal records, while 63% of executives report having hired someone with a conviction within the past year. These findings demonstrate that fair-chance hiring is becoming a mainstream workforce solution that balances business needs with public sentiment.[24]

Research consistently demonstrates that integrating justice-impacted individuals into work teams yields measurable organizational advantages. Beyond addressing labor shortages, this practice enhances overall productivity while cultivating a more collaborative and innovative workplace culture. Teams with JIP members often experience elevated morale and job satisfaction, leading to significantly lower turnover rates. Furthermore, companies recognized for their second chance hiring policies frequently gain a competitive edge in talent acquisition and creating customer loyalty.

Enhance Corporate Social Responsibility Profiles

Corporate social responsibility (CSR) has evolved from a philanthropic endeavor to a strategic driver of financial performance. Data reveals that purpose-driven organizations—those that authentically embed CSR into their core operations—outperform peers by a significant margin. Research indicates these companies experience growth rates 2.5 times faster than conventional businesses while generating superior equity returns.[25] This performance gap demonstrates that ethical business practices and profitability are not mutually exclusive, but rather mutually reinforcing.

Integrating JIPs into the workforce fulfills critical CSR goals while simultaneously strengthening brand perception as a socially conscious enterprise. This commitment to workforce inclusion resonates powerfully with modern consumers—Cone

Communications research shows 94% of Americans say domestic job growth is a top priority and 78% of Americans say they consider a company's social justice commitments when making purchasing decisions.[26] Companies embracing second chance hiring frequently gain additional benefits, including positive media coverage, public recognition, and enhanced brand differentiation—all of which amplify customer appeal in an increasingly values-driven marketplace. By aligning hiring practices with these demonstrated public values, businesses not only elevate their reputation among consumers and stakeholders but also secure a tangible competitive edge, turning social impact into commercial advantage.[27]

Consumer preferences for socially responsible companies directly translates to superior financial performance. Companies that invest in social impact initiatives consistently outperform competitors, achieving 20% higher revenue and 20% higher valuation compared to low purpose-driven brands.[28] A Nielsen global survey of 29,000 consumers reveals 50% will pay more for products from companies committed to social impact.[29] The financial benefits compound over time—businesses that forge emotional connections through meaningful initiatives see customer lifetime value increase up to 306% over five years.[30]

These findings demonstrate that CSR is not charity but a strategic driver of premium pricing, customer loyalty, and sustained revenue growth. Second chance hiring and integrating JIPs into workforce creates a win-win scenario: businesses gain a competitive edge in today's market, while simultaneously advancing economic growth.

85

CHAPTER 5

THE ECONOMIC THEORIES BEHIND SECOND CHANCE EMPLOYMENT

> "Whatever the mind of man can conceive and believe,
> it can achieve."
> —Oliver Napolean Hill, American author

The economic case for second chance employment extends far beyond moral arguments and empirical evidence—it is rooted in rigorous theoretical frameworks that demonstrate clear benefits for businesses, industries, and the broader economy. Foundational economic theories explain why investing in justice-impacted people is not just socially responsible but economically strategic. The Human Capital Theory reveals how education and skills training transform JIPs into productive contributors, while the Labor Market Segmentation Theory exposes the systemic barriers that confine them to unstable, low-wage jobs. The Social Capital and Network Theory further illustrates how incarceration dismantles professional and personal connections which impedes economic growth at both the individual and national level.

The theories are clear—when we educate and employ justice-impacted individuals, we are not just rehabilitating people; we are turning around distressed economic assets. This is undervalued human capital trapped beneath invisible barriers of prejudice and policy. Every time a business hesitates to hire someone with a record, they are not avoiding risk—they are forfeiting competitive advantage. This is not social work—it is the next frontier of human capital strategy.

Human Capital Theory

Economic theories provide a strong foundation for understanding why investing in JIPs is not just an act of social goodwill but a strategic move that benefits businesses, industries, and the broader economy. The Human Capital Theory (HCT), one of the most influential concepts in economic thought, posits that an individual's skills, knowledge, and experience—collectively referred to as human capital—are essential drivers of economic productivity and growth. Most importantly, the theory postulates that *any* individual can increase their productivity and economic value through investment in education, skills, and experience. First articulated by Adam Smith and refined in the 1960s by Nobel laureate economists Gary Becker and Theodore Schultz, HCT demonstrates how investments in human capital yield dividends for both individuals and the broader economy.

When applied to justice-impacted individuals, the Human Capital Theory reveals a vast reservoir of untapped potential. Despite facing systemic barriers and social stigma, JIPs possess inherent capabilities that, when properly cultivated, can generate significant economic value. Targeted investments in education and skills training transform this potential into tangible workforce assets. Numerous studies illustrate that education and training programs equip individuals with the skills needed to secure stable employment, reintegrate into society and reduce recidivism. As cited earlier, a study from the RAND Corporation reports that inmates who participate in educational programs while incarcerated are 43% less likely to return to prison within three years of release compared to those who do not participate in such programs.[1]

The economic benefits of developing JIPs' human capital extend well beyond lowered incarceration rates. The Brookings Institution reports that formerly incarcerated individuals with higher levels of education and training have higher lifetime earnings, leading to increased consumer spending, higher tax revenues, and reduced reliance on social welfare programs.[2] These effects create a virtuous cycle of economic participation and growth.

Industries experiencing critical labor shortages stand to gain significant advantage from this approach. Sectors like construction, manufacturing, and technology—persistently challenged by skilled worker deficits—can address their talent gaps by investing in JIP training initiatives. Programs like The Last Mile, which prepares incarcerated individuals for careers in software development, prove that with proper training and support, JIPs can excel in high-demand fields while delivering exceptional value to employers.

The societal returns on these investments are equally significant. Human capital investments yield cascading benefits:

stronger families, more vibrant communities, and reduced strain on public resources traditionally allocated to criminal justice systems. The resulting savings can be redirected to education, healthcare, and infrastructure, creating a multiplier effect throughout the economy.

The long-term implications are profound. Children of incarcerated parents face heightened risk of poverty, trauma, and education disruption. Successful workforce integration of JIPs not only helps break this intergenerational cycle of poverty and incarceration but creates pathways to prosperity for future generations. As demographic shifts tighten labor markets, the strategic importance of developing this talent pool will only intensify. JIPs represent not just an untapped resource, but a critical component of America's future workforce competitiveness.

The Human Capital Theory makes the economic case clear: justice-impacted individuals possess the same capacity for skill development and productivity enhancement as any other workforce segment. By providing education, training, and employment opportunities, we unlock human potential that would otherwise remain dormant. The result is a stronger economy, better positioned to meet the challenges of the 21st century. This approach transforms human capital theory from academic concept to a practical solution, demonstrating how strategic investments in marginalized populations can yield extraordinary economic and social dividends. The data, the theory, and the practical outcomes all point to the same conclusion: when we invest in justice-impacted individuals, we invest in America's economic future.

Labor Market Segmentation

The theory of labor market segmentation (LMS) provides a critical framework for understanding how structural barriers prevent justice-impacted individuals from achieving their full economic potential, regardless of their skills or qualifications. Developed in the 1970s by economists Michael Piore and Peter Doeringer, the LMS theory reveals how modern economies are divided into distinct labor tiers that operate under fundamentally different rules and reward systems. The primary labor market offers stable employment with living wages, benefits, and opportunities for advancement, while the secondary labor market traps workers in precarious, low-wage jobs with little security or upward mobility. For JIPs, this segmentation creates particularly devastating consequences, as societal stigma and institutional barriers systematically exclude them from primary market opportunities despite their human capital potential.

The mechanisms enforcing this exclusion are both overt and subtle. Many employers maintain blanket bans on hiring individuals with criminal records, regardless of offense type, rehabilitation, or job relevance. Professional licensing designations restrict JIPs from hundreds of occupations, while background check policies disproportionately filter out qualified candidates.

These barriers create what economists call "statistical discrimination," where employers make hiring decisions based on perceived differences—group level stereotypes—rather than individual merit. As a result, JIPs are disproportionately represented in temporary, low-paying, precarious jobs with little job security and few opportunities for advancement.[3]

The economic consequences of this systemic exclusion are pervasive. When JIPs with skills are prevented from contributing at their full capacity, they find themselves in a cycle of underemployment, leading to lower earnings, general discontentment, and a higher likelihood of returning to criminal activity due to financial instability. Additionally, the size of the JIP talent pool trapped in the secondary labor market constrains overall economic growth.

Second chance employment initiatives are crucial in bridging the gap between the segmented labor markets through three proven strategies. First, create sector-specific training programs that align JIP skills with high-demand occupations facing worker shortages. By providing JIPs with the targeted training and credentials, they overcome the barriers that traditionally confined them to the secondary labor market. Second, utilize individualized assessments to mitigate unintended background check filtering and allow candidates to demonstrate their qualifications. Third, offer transitional support services to address the unique challenges JIPs encounter when entering primary market positions. Transportation assistance, mentorship programs, and financial coaching help overcome practical barriers while helping

JIPs transition into the primary labor market and build sustainable careers.

Ultimately, labor market segmentation represents one of the most persistent yet solvable inefficiencies in modern economies. By implementing evidence-based reforms that connect JIPs with primary market opportunities, the United States can simultaneously address workforce shortages, boost economic productivity, and reduce recidivism—a rare policy trifecta where societal imperatives align perfectly with economic self-interest. For JIPs, it means access to better jobs, higher wages, and greater financial security. For employers, it means access to a motivated and loyal workforce eager to contribute to the organization's success. For society, it means safer communities, lower social welfare costs, and a more productive economy that increases GDP. The challenge is not identifying solutions, but mustering the collective will to dismantle artificial barriers that serve no productive purpose. As labor markets continue evolving in response to demographic shifts and technological change, the integration of justice-impacted talent will become not just an equity issue, but an economic necessity for maintaining global competitiveness.

The Social Capital & Network Theory

The conceptual framework of social capital emerged through the groundbreaking work of French sociologist Pierre Bourdieu during the 1970s. Bourdieu's seminal theoretical contributions first defined social capital as the aggregate of actual or potential resources linked to possession of relationships. In the following decades, economist James Coleman expanded the framework demonstrating how social connections facilitate human capital development, and political scientist Robert Putnam revealed its power to enable collective economic action. Together, these scholars established social capital as the invisible architecture of opportunity—the trust, reciprocity, and information sharing embedded in professional and community networks that individuals leverage for economic advancement.

Simply put, social capital refers to the benefits individuals receive from their social networks. These connections function as powerful conduits for opportunity, particularly in employment contexts. Individuals with well-developed social networks benefit from a hidden advantage—they receive timely information about unadvertised positions, credible endorsements that bypass formal screening processes, and ongoing support throughout their careers. Those embedded in robust networks often underestimate this advantage, treating their connections as natural rather than recognizing them as a form of privilege that shapes career trajectories. This reality creates an invisible divide between those who can leverage relationships for economic mobility and those whose networks have been fractured by circumstance or systemic exclusion.[4,5]

The moment an individual encounters the criminal justice system—whether through an arrest, a formal charge, or a DOJ press release—their social capital begins to collapse. This damage occurs irrespective of actual guilt or outcome. The mere accusation triggers social capital destruction. Despite the due process principle of being "innocent until proven guilty," media coverage about the accusations and charges create an indelible perception of guilt—accusation alone permanently impairs social capital.

The damage to social capital compounds exponentially as an individual endures the justice system's protracted timeline—the time to progress through the criminal justice process and return to society. There are three distinct phases an individual must endure: pretrial, incarceration, and probation/supervised release.

In the pretrial phase, the average case processing time is 6.5 months for a misdemeanor case and 8.5 months for a felony case. Should an individual choose to fight for their innocence at trial, the time balloons to between 12 and 36 months. During this limbo period of up to three years, professional connections atrophy, personal relationships fracture, and digital footprints of allegations solidify.[6,7] If convicted and imprisoned, an individual will likely join the 63% of inmates sentenced between 5 to 20 years.[8] Then, after release from prison, the individual will be under federal supervision—also known as probation—for anywhere from one year to five years.

Using averages across the three phases—pre-trial, incarceration, and probation—an individual's journey through the criminal justice system takes on average fourteen years. That is fourteen years of government prosecution and oversight. Fourteen years of legal defense expenses and court fees. Fourteen years of entanglement, anxiety, and uncertainty. This fourteen-year time-span carries severe consequences when measured against societal benchmarks: it represents the duration needed to complete both undergraduate and doctoral education, it encompasses two full business cycles in the modern economy, and it spans the complete technological transformation of most industries. Yet during this same period, JIPs experience systematic exclusion from these developmental pathways. Their human capital depreciates as skills grow obsolete and their professional networks dissolve from disuse. The system's lengthy grip creates the ultimate paradox—individuals emerge from their "debt to society" only to find themselves permanently behind, having been denied the very tools and connections needed for successful reintegration.

Even after completing probation, JIPS face immense barriers to rebuilding their social networks and professional connections. The combined effects of extended absence from the community, permanent online reputational damage from media coverage, and persistent social stigma create a perfect storm of exclusion that continues long after formal supervision ends. The result is perpetual marginalization—where the official completion of a sentence fails to restore one's standing in social and economic spheres. This ongoing exclusion persists despite evidence of rehabilitation, creating structural headwinds requiring extraordinary efforts and institutional support to rebuild professional networks.

Compounding the challenge of severed networks, many JIPs face the additional burden of returning to economically distressed communities—neighborhoods suffering from depleted job prospects, underfunded workforce development programs, and sparse professional networks, creating a geographic poverty trap. The spatial isolation from economic hubs means even motivated JIPs encounter physical barriers to opportunity, with limited access to employers, mentors, or training facilities that could facilitate upward mobility.[9]

Social capital operates as the critical bridge between incarceration and meaningful reintegration. Justice-impacted individuals face the destruction of relationships at every phase—from the initial allegations through incarceration through years of supervision—leaving them essentially stranded. This deprivation proves particularly devastating when compounded by geographic disadvantages and digital permanence. Yet the inverse is equally true: targeted interventions that restore professional connections, rebuild community ties, and provide network-rich environments demonstrate remarkable success. Human capital alone cannot overcome social capital deficits. True rehabilitation requires investing not just in skills training, but in the relational infrastructure that transforms potential into opportunity.[10]

CHAPTER 6

LEARNING FROM GLOBAL INITIATIVES

"If I have seen further, it is by standing on the shoulders of giants."
—Sir Issac Newton, mathematician, astronomer, and author

Comparative analysis of criminal justice systems worldwide demonstrates a consistent pattern—nations prioritizing rehabilitation over punitive measures consistently achieve superior outcomes in both reintegration and public safety. The various models provide actionable blueprints for transforming workforce development strategies. Particularly instructive are programs that align correctional education with labor market demands, creating pipelines of job-ready talent upon release. These approaches prove that economic growth and public safety are not competing priorities, but mutually reinforcing objectives when systems invest in human potential.

In Europe, Scandinavian correctional systems exemplify how humane treatment combined with comprehensive education programs fosters successful reintegration. While Germany developed prison-based vocational training programs jointly with manufacturing unions to produce certified skilled workers, demonstrating the power of public-private partnerships. In the southern hemisphere, New Zealand's justice system incorporates indigenous Māori concepts of restorative justice, creating processes that simultaneously hold offenders accountable while repairing community relationships. Meanwhile, Canada's correctional education initiatives, particularly in technology fields, equip inmates with in-demand skills for the modern economy.

Across cultures and legal systems, varied approaches achieve measurable success to reduce recidivism and transform JIPs into productive workers. The results challenge long-held assumptions about punishment and public safety while simultaneously offering practical models to address labor shortages. By examining these international examples, the United States can identify transferable strategies that balance societal protection with economic opportunity.

Global Rehabilitation Philosophies

Incarceration and rehabilitation philosophies differ greatly globally depending on cultural, social, and historical norms. At one end of the philosophical spectrum, rehabilitative systems focus on transforming offenders into productive citizens. At the other end of the spectrum, punitive justice systems are primarily designed to inflict penalties on offenders to deter crime through the fear of punishment.

During the 1990s, Norway and Sweden pioneered a radical transformation of their penal systems, replacing punitive approaches with a restorative justice model centered on rehabilitation. This paradigm shift reconceived incarceration as an opportunity for personal transformation rather than mere punishment.

Correctional facilities were redesigned as educational environments emphasizing skill-building, cognitive behavioral therapy, and community reintegration preparation. Norway's sustained investment in prisoner education, vocational training, and humane living conditions has produced one of the world's most dramatic recidivism reductions—from 70% to under 20% over two decades.[1]

In contrast, several Islamic nations incorporate Sharia law as a foundational element of their criminal justice systems, which operate on philosophical principles that emphasize retribution (qisas) and deterrence (ta'zir) as primary responses to crime. Countries including Saudi Arabia and Iran implement fixed penalties prescribed by the Quran. Crimes like theft and adultery may incur punishments like amputation or flogging.

Amid varying criminal justice philosophies, the United States occupies a complex middle ground, embodying an ongoing tension between punitive and rehabilitative approaches. Historically following a punitive approach rooted in the idea of deterrence and incapacitation, the U.S. criminal justice system emphasizes punishment as a means of preventing future crimes. Characterized by long prison sentences, mandatory minimums, and limited opportunities for parole, punitive justice systems are designed to inflict penalties on offenders. However, over the past fifteen years, the United States has embraced a more rehabilitative stance, as data indicates that restorative justice leads to better outcomes for the individual and society.

Case Study 1: The Nordic Approach

Countries like Norway and Sweden focus on rehabilitation, education, and reintegration, creating a supportive environment that prepares JIPs for successful reentry. Both countries are renowned for their open prison system, which is designed to resemble life outside of incarceration as closely as possible. Inmates are housed in facilities with fewer physical barriers and are granted more freedom and responsibility. For instance, Bastoy Prison in Norway is situated on an island and is often described as the world's nicest prison. Inmates live in small cottages and participate in constructive programming, agricultural work, and other forms of productive labor.[2]

Similarly, in Sweden, Österåker is an open prison facility allowing inmates to live in conditions that closely mirror normal life. These prisons grant trust and autonomy to individuals while emphasizing educational programs, vocational training, and work opportunities to foster personal development and skill acquisition. Inmates can leave the facility during the day for work or education, returning only for the night.[3] The idea is to gradually prepare inmates for life after prison and reduce the psychological impact of incarceration. These open prisons account for a significant proportion of the prison population in Nordic countries, with nearly one-third of Sweden's prison population housed in such facilities.[4]

A central tenet of the Nordic incarceration model is the emphasis on human rights and dignity. The philosophy behind this approach is that the deprivation of liberty is punishment enough, and additional punitive measures are neither necessary nor effective.[5] This principle shapes the prison environment, where humane conditions are prioritized and the use of solitary confinement and physical restraints is minimized.

This commitment to human dignity continues through the reentry process. Inmates are encouraged to maintain family connections, participate in social activities, and engage in meaningful education/work programs. This comprehensive approach ensures individuals emerge better prepared to contribute to society than when they entered. The preparation for reentry is seen not just as a benefit to the individual but as a crucial element in reducing recidivism and enhancing public safety.[6]

The Scandinavian approach to rehabilitation rests on three fundamental pillars: comprehensive education, practical vocational training, and structured social reintegration. Norway's system mandates personalized development plans for incarcerated individuals, mapping their educational and professional growth throughout their sentence. The academic offerings span from foundational literacy programs to accredited university courses, enabling many prisoners to earn degrees while serving their sentences. This educational framework extends beyond classroom learning to include hands-on vocational preparation in trades like construction, culinary arts, and automotive repair. These programs are designed not as privileges but as essential components of rehabilitation, equipping participants with tangible skills for successful reintegration.[7]

Sweden's rehabilitation model mirrors Norway's, with education and vocational training at its core. The Swedish Prison and Probation Service offers diverse programs designed to equip inmates with practical skills and improve their employability. These include apprenticeships with local businesses and organizations, providing inmates valuable real-world experience and opportunities to build professional networks before release. This approach ensures prisoners develop not just job skills but meaningful connections to support their transition back into society.

Norway and Sweden have pioneered holistic reintegration programs that begin during incarceration and extend for years after release. These initiatives provide structured support across housing placements, gainful employment, and community reconnection. The success of these programs is evident in the high employment rates among former inmates, with over 70% of released individuals in Norway finding employment within two years.[8] What distinguishes the Nordic approach is its recognition of rehabilitation as an ongoing process. Programs include essential mental health services and counseling to address root causes of criminal behavior, combining practical support with psychological care. This dual focus on external stability and internal transformation explains the region's exceptional success in reducing recidivism and fostering productive reintegration.

Recidivism rates serve as the critical benchmark for evaluating criminal justice systems, and the Nordic countries' exceptional outcomes demonstrate the power of their rehabilitation-focused approach. Norway maintains one of the world's lowest reoffending rates at approximately 20%, while Sweden achieves a similarly impressive 30% rate.[9,10] The Scandinavian experience proves that when correctional systems prioritize human development over punishment, they create safer communities through genuine behavioral change rather than temporary incapacitation.

While the Nordic correctional model carries higher upfront costs—approximately $126,000 annually per individual compared to $46,000 in the U.S.[11]—this investment yields substantial long-term savings. The superficial cost differential reflects a fundamentally different philosophy where traditional systems emphasize containment, the Nordic approach invests in human capital development. This proactive strategy generates compounding returns through dramatically lower recidivism, reducing overall prison expenditures and societal costs of crime—including law enforcement, judicial proceedings, and social welfare burdens.[12] The model's demonstrated success has sparked growing international interest, particularly among nations grappling with overcrowded prisons and high recidivism rates. By transforming correctional facilities into centers of rehabilitation rather than mere warehouses of punishment, the Nordic countries have created a sustainable system that balances fiscal responsibility with measurable improvements in public safety and social welfare.

Case Study 2: The German Way

Similarly to the Scandinavian system, Germany's incarceration model is rooted in the belief that rehabilitation is essential to public safety and social reintegration. The German Federal Constitutional Court established that public safety is not achieved through incarceration, but rather through the successful rehabilitation and reintegration of offenders into society.[13] At the heart of this approach lies an extensive vocational training system integrated throughout German correctional facilities. Available data indicates approximately 75% of incarcerated individuals participate in vocational or employment programs during their sentences. These initiatives range from traditional trades to advanced technical training, all designed to provide marketable skills for post-release employment.[14,15]

The German correctional system offers comprehensive vocational training programs in high-demand fields including carpentry, plumbing, electrical systems, and culinary arts. These industry-aligned programs combine classroom instruction with hands-on workshops that replicate authentic work environments, all supervised by qualified professionals. The curriculum meets Germany's rigorous apprenticeship standards, ensuring participants earn certifications recognized nationwide.[16]

This skills development is enhanced by robust support services including job placement assistance, mentorship programs, and employment counseling to create a seamless transition from incarceration to workforce participation. By equipping JIPs with both technical competencies and professional support, the system provides employers with skilled workers while giving JIPs the tools for economic stability.

Germany has legally mandated that all incarcerated individuals have access to educational and vocational opportunities.[17] This commitment was further strengthened in 2014 when Germany became the first nation to grant prisoners the right to unionize, enabling them to advocate for fair wages and workplace protections. A Federal Ministry of Justice follow up study revealed that 66% of vocational program participants remained crime-free for at least three years post-release.[14]

Germany's vocational training programs stand out for its deep integration with the private sector, creating a direct pipeline from incarceration to employment. The correctional system partners with local businesses to develop apprenticeship programs where inmates gain practical experience under the supervision of industry professionals. These collaborations often take the form of part-time work placements or formal apprenticeships in fields ranging from automotive repair to advanced manufacturing.

A particularly successful model operates in Baden-Württemberg, where correctional facilities partner with automotive firms to provide inmates certified training in vehicle maintenance that frequently result in formal job offers upon the participants release.[18] This synergy between prisons and employers yields remarkable results with 75% of program participants securing employment within six months of release.[19]

Access to stable employment following incarceration represents one of the most powerful deterrents against reoffending. Germany's data demonstrates that the recidivism rate for individuals who complete vocational training programs is just 30%—a remarkable 40% reduction compared to those without such training.[20] These results underscore how skills development directly disrupts the recidivism cycle by addressing its root cause—economic insecurity.[21]

Germany's correctional system demonstrates how vocational training and comprehensive reintegration programs can successfully transform inmates into productive citizens. By providing justice-impacted individuals with marketable skills aligned with labor market needs and ongoing reentry support, these initiatives dramatically lower recidivism rates while creating a pipeline of skilled workers for the economy.

The model's effectiveness stems from its focus on practical, employer-recognized training combined with real workplace experience. This rehabilitation-focused system delivers measurable societal returns by enhancing public safety through recidivism reduction, economic growth through workforce participation, and strengthened communities through a higher labor participation rate. Germany's experience offers compelling evidence that investing in human capital development during incarceration produces long-term dividends in both social stability and economic productivity.

Case Study 3: New Zealand Restorative Justice

New Zealand has pioneered a distinctive approach to criminal justice by weaving indigenous Māori restorative traditions into its legal framework. Unlike conventional European systems, New Zealand emphasizes communal conflict resolution through processes that prioritize healing over punishment. This model brings together victims, offenders, and community members in dialogue-focused resolutions aimed at repairing harm rather than exacting retribution.

The system's innovative power lies in its holistic understanding of crime's impact—recognizing how offenses damage victims, disrupt communities, and diminish offenders themselves. By addressing these multidimensional harms through a face-to-face accountability process, New Zealand achieves higher victim satisfaction and lower recidivism rates than traditional punitive approaches. The process is typically facilitated through structured conferences that bring together victims, offenders, and their support networks in a voluntary dialogue. These carefully facilitated gatherings create space for victims to articulate the full impact of the harm they experienced, while allowing offenders to directly acknowledge responsibility for their actions.

The process emphasizes authentic accountability through collaboratively determined reparations—which may include personalized apologies, community service, or other meaningful actions tailored to address the specific harm caused. By focusing on reconciliation rather than mere punishment, these conferences transform justice from an abstract state action into a tangible, human-centered process of healing and restoration.[22]

New Zealand's restorative justice approach delivers proven results across two critical metrics: recidivism reduction and victim healing. Ministry of Justice data reveals that offenders participating in restorative conferences demonstrate 20% lower recidivism rates compared to those processed through traditional courts—clear evidence of the model's rehabilitative effectiveness.[23]

The system achieves equally impressive outcomes for victims, with over 80% reporting satisfaction with the process's fairness and their opportunity to voice the crime's full impact. Beyond procedural justice, these conferences facilitate emotional healing, as many victims describe the face-to-face dialogue as transformative to their recovery journey. Together, these outcomes demonstrate how New Zealand's victim-centered approach achieves what punitive systems often fail to deliver—meaningful accountability that reduces future harm while addressing past trauma.[24]

New Zealand's innovative integration of Māori restorative traditions into its justice system presents a compelling alternative to conventional punitive approaches. By centering on harm repair rather than retribution, this model achieves significantly lower recidivism rates, delivers unprecedented victim satisfaction, and rebuilds fractured community connections. These outcomes position New Zealand's approach as a blueprint for jurisdictions seeking to move beyond punishment toward a justice system that truly transforms lives and strengthens communities.

Case Study 4: The Canadian Strategy

Looking closer to home, Canada has been progressively incorporating technology and higher education into its prison rehabilitation programs, recognizing the pivotal role that education and skill development play in reducing recidivism and facilitating successful reintegration into society.

The Canadian correctional system has implemented several initiatives, including the "Prison Education Project," which seeks to provide inmates with access to post-secondary education through partnerships with Canadian universities and colleges. This program allows inmates to enroll in various online courses, ranging from basic literacy to university-level business, social sciences, and information technology courses. These courses are delivered through a secure online platform, enabling inmates to pursue their studies while serving their sentences.[25]

Building on its academic programs, Canada has implemented cutting-edge digital skills training to prepare inmates for the modern workforce. Initiatives like "Tech For Good" offer intensive training in high-demand technical fields including computer programming and web design. These programs do more than teach coding languages—they cultivate essential cognitive skills like analytical thinking, creative problem-solving, and logical reasoning that transfer across professions.[26]

Combining higher education with technology training allows participants to emerge with both technical competencies and renewed self-confidence. By focusing on both technical proficiency and personal development, this approach tackles the full range of reintegration challenges—giving individuals marketable expertise while rebuilding the soft skills they need to succeed after release. The model demonstrates how targeted digital education can convert prison time into a period of career preparation and personal growth.

Research demonstrates that individuals who engage in educational programs experience positive behavioral changes and have lower rates of disciplinary infractions while incarcerated. This personal growth extends beyond prison walls, as education empowers inmates to envision a future beyond crime and incarceration. By acquiring new skills and knowledge, inmates gain the confidence and motivation to pursue legitimate employment and contribute positively to society.[27] A review of the Victoria University post-secondary prisoner education program revealed a recidivism rate of just 14%, compared with 52% for non-participants.[28] The same study reported participants demonstrated social, cognitive, and behavioral change.[27]

Canadian universities have been instrumental in providing education opportunities to incarcerated individuals. Leading institutions like the University of Toronto, the University of Ottawa, and Athabasca University have created specialized programs that address the distinct challenges faced by prison-based learners. These initiatives feature adaptable learning structures, enabling students to progress at their own pace while receiving dedicated academic support. By offering accredited courses, these universities ensure that incarcerated learners earn meaningful credentials—opening doors to continued education and career opportunities upon reintegration into society.[29]

Leading technology companies have become vital collaborators in prison education initiatives as well, offering cutting-edge training, resources, and industry expertise to help incarcerated individuals build competitive digital skills. For example, Microsoft Canada has partnered with the Correctional Service of Canada to deliver specializing training programs in cloud computing, cybersecurity, and data analytics. These initiatives are specifically designed to equip participants with job-ready technical competencies, positioning them for employment in Canada's rapidly expanding tech sector—where demand for skilled workers continues to outpace supply.[30]

These innovative alliances between correctional institutions, universities, and technology leaders demonstrate Canada's progressive, multi-sector approach to rehabilitation and recidivism reduction. By leveraging the expertise and resources of these partners, Canada provides justice-impacted individuals with the education and skills needed to succeed in today's competitive job market, ultimately contributing to safer communities and a more productive society.

Adopt The Best

The United States does not need to start from scratch—proven solutions already exist. Across the U.S. and internationally, innovative programs demonstrate how investing in incarcerated individuals leads to measurable benefits for workers, communities, and the broader economy. Rather than reinvent the wheel, the United States must simply replicate and scale these successful models to catalyze this underutilized workforce.

Even the United Kingdom, which incarcerates more people than any other Western European nation, has proven that prison workforce initiatives can deliver exceptional results. The UK Ministry of Justice established the New Futures Network (NFN) to facilitate partnerships between prisons and employers, creating pathways to stable employment for JIPs. The NFN analyzes labor market needs and designs targeted training programs in high-demand sectors like construction, logistics and manufacturing. As of 2021, NFN had facilitated employment opportunities for over 5,000 individuals across the UK, with many employers reporting high levels of satisfaction with the quality of work provided by former inmates. Notably, participants in NFN programs have shown significantly lower recidivism rates compared to the national average, with a 34% reduction in recidivism among those who secured employment through the network.[31]

Scaling a program like NFN in the U.S. would involve establishing similar partnerships between correctional facilities and industries experiencing worker shortages. Given the size and diversity of the U.S. economy, this model could be tailored to different regions, focusing on sectors crucial to local economies. Manufacturing-heavy states might partner with automotive or aerospace firms, while tech-centric areas could prioritize coding and IT certifications.

From Norway's open prisons to Germany's vocational training and Canada's tech-education partnerships, rehabilitation-focused criminal justice systems yield transformative benefits—lower recidivism, stronger communities, and a more skilled workforce. These models prove that treating incarceration as an opportunity for education and reintegration, rather than mere punishment, fosters long-term societal and economic gains.

The contrast between rehabilitation and traditional punitive approaches presents a critical choice: keep investing in costly, ineffective cycles of incarceration, or adopt evidence-based strategies that prioritize human potential. Vocational training, restorative justice, and technology education not only equip individuals for gainful employment but also address labor shortages and strengthen economies.

For nations like the United States, the path forward is clear. By integrating the most effective elements of global rehabilitation models, policymakers can build a system that enhances public safety while unlocking economic opportunity. The success of these international examples is not theoretical; it is measurable and replicable. The question is no longer whether rehabilitation works, but how quickly the United States can implement it. Ultimately, criminal justice reform is not just about fairness or equality—it is a pragmatic investment in a more productive so-ciety. The world's best practices provide a blueprint; the next step is action.

CHAPTER 7

POLICY, ADVOCACY, AND THE PATH FORWARD

"Without deviation from the norm, progress is not possible."
—Frank Zappa, American composer & musician

As illustrated in the data, employment challenges facing justice-impacted people represent not only a social issue but also a significant economic opportunity. Despite evidence that gainful employment reduces recidivism, current systems and persistent policy gaps often create unnecessary barriers to workforce participation. This disconnect between policy and outcomes undermines both economic potential and public safety.

While initiatives like Ban the Box and the Fair Chance Act have made progress, many current approaches still fall short in addressing the interconnected challenges that perpetuate cycles of unemployment. Strategic policy interventions—from occupational licensing reforms to targeted hiring incentives—can help bridge these gaps, meeting workforce demands while lowering societal costs.

By adopting standardized metrics, expanding proven programs, and eliminating counterproductive barriers, the United States can create a system where successful rehabilitation translates directly into economic contribution. The stakes extend far beyond individual hiring decisions or even recidivism reduction—this is about shaping the future of economic growth and public safety across the nation.

Systemic Challenges Faced by JIPs

Justice-impacted individuals face substantial employment barriers, including pervasive stigma and restrictive legal regulations which collectively contribute to disproportionately high unemployment rates. A significant barrier is the pervasive stigma attached to having a criminal record. Employer reluctance remains a persistent challenge with 47% of employers unwilling to hire JIPs due to perceptional concerns about workplace safety, legal liability, and reputational risk.[1] This discrimination persists despite empirical data demonstrating that JIPs are no more likely to commit workplace crime than other employees, highlighting a critical disconnect between perception and reality.[2]

Legal and regulatory barriers also pose significant challenges. In the United States, nearly 25% of jobs require a government-issued license, and many states have blanket bans on granting these licenses to individuals with criminal records, regardless of the offense's nature or the time elapsed since the conviction.[3] These barriers disproportionately affect minorities, who are overrepresented in the criminal justice system, thereby exacerbating racial inequalities in employment.

Additionally, correctional systems frequently fail to provide adequate educational or vocational training, leaving many JIPs without the qualifications needed to compete in today's demanding labor market. Despite research from RAND Corporation showing that state prisoners in educational programs often face outdated curricula misaligned with current job market demands, the return on investment remains encouraging—data indicates that for every \$1 invested in prison education, taxpayers save, on average, between \$4 and \$5 in three-year incarceration costs. Targeted investments in education yield incredible results.[4]

Current Policy Landscape

For JIPs the legal and systemic hurdles to gainful employment are pervasive and often insurmountable, creating a cycle of disadvantages that persist for their entire life—long after their sentence has been served. The barriers begin with the criminal record itself, which acts as a permanent scarlet letter in a world where background checks are standard hiring protocol. According to the Society for Human Resource Management (SHRM), over 90% of employers conduct criminal background checks—which automatically disqualify applicants with criminal records, regardless of the nature of the offense or the time elapsed since the conviction.[5]

One of the most prominent policies to address the issue is the *Ban the Box* initiative, which has been adopted by more than 35 states and over 150 municipalities across the United States.[6] This policy prohibits employers from asking about a candidate's criminal history on initial job applications. However, while Ban the

Box increases interview opportunities for applicants with criminal records at the outset, most Ban the Box policies do not prevent an employer from conducting background checks later in the hiring process. This generally results in a rejection once their criminal record comes to light—wasting effort and time for both parties. The policy's limitations become especially apparent in states without complementary fair-chance laws.

In jurisdictions lacking additional protections, employers often use the delayed disclosure as a screening tool rather than an opportunity for meaningful consideration. As a result, Ban the Box on its own fails to address the deeper systemic barriers justice-impacted individuals face when seeking employment. To fulfill its promise, Ban the Box must be implemented alongside three critical support pillars: laws requiring individualized assessments of criminal records, robust record-clearing mechanisms, and incentives for employers to hire and retain justice-impacted workers. Without a comprehensive approach, the removal of the conviction checkbox is merely symbolic, leaving systemic employment barriers fundamentally unchanged.

While Ban the Box represents an important first step in criminal justice reform, the Fair Chance Act represents a critical evolution towards implementing a robust framework for hiring JIPs. Pioneered in California and New York, this legislation establishes crucial protections that go beyond simply removing the criminal history checkbox from job applications. The Fair Chance Act's most significant provision requires employers to postpone all background checks until after extending a conditional job offer. This fundamental shift in hiring timelines gives JIPs the opportunity to first demonstrate their qualifications and skills rather than being screened out immediately based on their past. Additionally, and perhaps more importantly, the Act mandates that employers conduct an individualized assessment considering factors such as the nature of the offense, the time elapsed since the conviction, and evidence of rehabilitation.[7]

While policies like Ban the Box and the Fair Chance Act represent important progress, their inconsistent implementation across states and industries creates new challenges. The current regulatory landscape remains fragmented, with varying standards that confuse both employers and job seekers. JIPs often struggle to understand their rights when protections differ by jurisdiction, while employers face compliance difficulties when operating across multiple regions with conflicting requirements. This lack of uniformity undermines the effectiveness of fair chance hiring policies and perpetuates systemic barriers to employment.[8]

Beyond good intentioned laws, occupational licensing restrictions present formidable legal barriers for JIPs seeking meaningful employment. With one in four jobs nationally requiring government-issued licenses, these regulations have an outsized impact on economic mobility. The restrictions prove particularly exclusionary in sectors like healthcare and education—fields where qualified candidates are routinely rejected based solely on their past rather than their present capabilities. The cumulative effect excludes JIPs from entire sectors of the economy, limiting their job prospects to low-wage, low-skill positions with little room for advancement.[9]

Even in industries where JIPs are legally permitted to work, invisible barriers persist through corporate policies and insurance restrictions. Many employers—deterred by concerns over liability, workplace safety, and reputational risk—voluntarily impose exclusionary hiring practices. These barriers become particularly acute when insurance providers explicitly deny coverage for employees with criminal records, creating financial disincentives for employers. Industries involving vulnerable populations (childcare), high-value assets (transportation), or hazardous work environments (construction) frequently implement these exclusionary practices, despite evidence that JIPs pose no greater risks in these fields.[10]

A criminal record triggers devastating ripple effects that extend far beyond employment to systematically deny JIPs of fundamental resources needed for stability. Housing providers—including public housing authorities and private landlords—routinely reject applicants based on background checks, shutting out entire families from safe shelter. The financial shockwaves continue with Social Security suspending payments during incarceration, depriving households of critical income.[11] When it comes to food, thirty-two states restrict convicted felons from receiving Supplemental Nutrition Assistance Program (SNAP)—food stamps and thirty-six states restrict convicted felons from receiving Temporary Assistance to Needy Families (TANF)—welfare.[12]

These interconnected sanctions create an inescapable poverty trap: without housing, families struggle to stay together; without nutrition assistance, health deteriorates; without income support, desperation grows. Even after serving their sentences, JIPs remain permanently punished through institutionalized exclusion from society's basic safety nets. Rather than facilitating rehabilitation, these policies manufacture the very conditions that drive recidivism, contradicting their purported goal of public safety.[13]

Policy Recommendations

Expanding employment opportunities for justice-impacted people requires a comprehensive multi-faceted approach—one that eliminates systemic barriers while actively fostering workforce integration. The following eight legislative and policy recommendations would materially improve employment outcomes for JIPs, strengthen communities, and drive economic growth:

1. **Introduce National Expungement Program**:

   The greatest obstacle preventing JIPs from becoming productive members of society and fully realizing their potential is not a lack of skills or motivation, it is the indelible mark of a criminal record that follows for their entire life after a sentence has been served.

Currently, only 12 states offer limited record-clearing options—and only for state convictions, not federal. The state expungement laws are fragmented, burdened by complex eligibility rules, prohibitively expensive to navigate, and the bureaucratic hurdles make the process inaccessible to most who qualify.[14] A National Automatic Expungement Program would transform this system by creating a clear, universal pathway to a second chance—unlocking significant economic benefits for individuals, employers, and the nation as a whole.

The most compelling evidence for automatic expungement comes from a landmark University of Michigan study *Expungement of Criminal Convictions*. Their research revealed that 99% of people who received expungements in Michigan had no subsequent convictions—not even minor offenses—within five years, demonstrating that they pose *less risk* than the average citizen. The economic benefits are equally striking: within just one year of receiving an expungement, a recipient's chance of being employed increases by 113% while experiencing a 22% rise in wages.[15]

A National Automatic Expungement Program would create a uniform, standardized process to clear criminal records at both state and federal levels. This program would include automatic expungement for qualifying non-violent offenses after a set crime-free waiting period.

2. Enact a Federal Fair Chance Act:

While a number of states have implemented Fair Chance laws, the absence of federal legislation has resulted in an inconsistent patchwork of policies that create unnecessary compliance challenges for businesses and hinder economic growth. A comprehensive Federal Fair Chance Act would implement clear, uniform standards nationwide, requiring employers to first assess candidates based on their qualifications and skills before conducting background checks, which would only occur after a conditional job offer is extended.

The law would also mandate individualized assessments that weigh factors such as the nature of the offense in relation to the job responsibilities, how much time has passed since the conviction, and any demonstrated rehabilitation. These simple but profound shifts would fundamentally transform opportunities for JIPs while providing businesses with access to an underutilized talent pool.

Fair chance hiring is not about compromising standards or forcing unqualified candidates in roles—it is about recognizing that people grow, and that outdated barriers should not eclipse skills. This commonsense approach ensures candidates are judged by their current capabilities, not past mistakes. Evidence shows that companies embracing fair chance policies improve employee retention, engagement, and performance.

Consider Checkr, the $5 billion background-check technology firm, as a powerful example of second chance hiring's potential. Over the past decade, the company has made fair chance hiring a priority—and the data reveals a compelling story. JIPs hired through their program have an astonishingly low attrition rate of just 5%, compared to 22% companywide. This trend is not incidental. Checkr's internal metrics show that second chance employees demonstrate 30% higher engagement and loyalty than their peers, shattering the misconception that past convictions predict workplace performance.[16] The company's commitment extends beyond just hiring. In 2021, Checkr formalized its dedication by pledging 1% of employee time, 1% of product resources, 1% of equity, and 1% of annual profits to fair chance initiatives.

Checkr's success reveals the broader truth that merit-based hiring—looking beyond JIP stigma—builds a stronger company. Fair chance hiring is not charity; it is a competitive advantage. As labor markets tighten and skill gaps widen, companies that overlook this talent pool are not just upholding arbitrary barriers, they are leaving performance on the table.

3. **Streamline the Work Opportunity Tax Credit (WOTC)**: The Work Opportunity Tax Credit (WOTC) represents a powerful but underutilized tool for encouraging businesses

to hire justice-impacted individuals. While the program currently offers employers up to $9,600 per eligible hire, its effectiveness is severely hampered by unnecessary bureaucratic complexity for the benefit received. To maximize WOTC's potential as a driver of second chance hiring, the following reforms should be implemented.

First, simplify the application process by reducing multi-agency requirements. The current system forces employers to navigate a multi-step certification process involving three separate agencies: the IRS, Department of Labor, and state workforce offices, with approvals taking 90-120 days. This excessive red tape particularly discourages small businesses—which employ 46% of private sector workers—from participating.[17]

Second, increase the tax credit to better reflect administrative and hiring costs. The current credit range of $2,400 up to $9,600 fails to meaningfully offset expenses related to hiring, training, and retention. Raising the maximum credit to $15,000 for entry-level positions and $30,000 for high wage roles would provide adequate compensation for employers' investments.

Third, accelerate the tax credit payment to address upfront costs. The current system delays reimbursement often arriving months after hiring creating a cash flow timing mismatch. Implementing immediate payments of 50% of the credit amount would offset onboarding expenses in real time.

Fourth, modernize the verification process by integrating with existing systems like E-Verify. Automated screening could reduce processing times from months to under two weeks, making the program more accessible.

A redesigned WOTC structure would maintain all current program benefits while making participation more attractive and feasible for employers of all sizes—transforming the WOTC from an underperforming program into an effective hiring incentive.

4. **Enhance the Federal Bond Program**:

The Federal Bonding Program holds immense promise for advancing second chance hiring. Since 1966, this initiative has provided employers with a *free*, zero-deductible fidelity bond of up to $25,000 for six months against an employee's potential dishonest acts—all while maintaining a mere 1% claims rate.[18] Despite the risk-free protection and 99% success rate, the program potential remains limited by low employer awareness and outdated coverage parameters.

To maximize this program's effectiveness as a catalyst for second chance hiring, three strategic enhancements should be implemented. First, increase the maximum bond amount to $100,000 to better align with modern compensation levels and provide meaningful protection for higher-wage positions. Second, extend coverage from six months to twelve months to match standard employee performance cycles. Third, digitally integrate the application process with major hiring platforms and state workforce systems to streamline approval times and scale accessibility.

These practical yet powerful reforms would elevate the Federal Bonding Program from a well-kept secret to a standard hiring practice—giving employers across all industries the confidence to tap into an overlooked pool of talented workers.

5. **Create a Federal Reentry Employment Task Force**:
The fragmented system of employment initiatives and reentry services presents an extraordinary opportunity to create employment pathways for JIPs while unlocking significant economic potential. Currently, more than two dozen federal programs across multiple agencies operate in disconnected silos—from the Department of Labor's job training initiatives to the Department of Housing and Urban Development's housing assistance programs—squandering resources and severely limiting their collective impact.

The solution lies in creating a Federal Reentry Employment Task Force (FRETF)—a centralized body with the authority to align policies, eliminate redundancies, and drive measurable results. This coordinated approach would fundamentally transform this disparate patchwork system of well-intentioned but disconnected programs into a streamlined, results-oriented system. By breaking down agency silos and creating clear pathways from incarceration to employment,

FRETF could realize the full potential of existing investments while opening new avenues of economic mobility for millions of capable workers currently excluded from opportunity.

6. **Reform Occupational Licensing Laws**:

Occupational licensing requirements—which govern approximately 25% of U.S. jobs—have become one of the most pervasive yet overlooked barriers to economic mobility for justice-impacted persons.[19] Across professions ranging from barbers to nursing, blanket bans and vague "moral character" clauses routinely disqualify qualified candidates based on past convictions rather than current competencies. These restrictions disproportionately impact high-demand fields where JIPs could thrive such as construction jobs, education-related roles, and healthcare support occupations.

This broken system demands three concrete reforms. First, states must replace blanket bans with individualized assessments that properly evaluate the relevance of an offense to the specific job duties, the time elapsed since conviction, and verifiable proof of rehabilitation such as training certifications or employer recommendations. Second, implementing a formal "pre-clearance" process would create transparency for candidates to confirm their eligibility before investing substantial time and money in training programs. Third, automatic sunset provisions should be instituted to lift restrictions after 3 years for non-violent offenses and a longer time period for violent offenses. This recognizes that people can and do change, while reserving continued scrutiny for situations that genuinely warrant it.

Occupational licensing barriers represent a solvable injustice that denies thousands of qualified individuals a fair shot at meaningful careers. By implementing individualized assessments, pre-clearance processes, and automatic sunset provisions, the United States can create a system that values both public safety and human potential. These reforms would open doors to stable, skilled professions while maintaining rigorous standards—proving that smart policy can both expand opportunity and strengthen the economy.

7. **Increase Education and Vocational Training Funding**:

Education and vocational training serve as a transformative tool in preparing justice-impacted individuals to reenter society and contribute to GDP growth. The restoration of the Pell Grant for incarcerated students in 2024 marked a watershed moment for prison education, reversing a 30-year ban that had denied thousands of JIPs access to higher learning. While this policy change could empower approximately 760,000 individuals annually with degrees and certifications, it represents just the first step in addressing systemic gaps in prison education and vocational training.[20]

Despite its transformative powers, the roll out of Pell Grant certified prison education programs has been slow to materialize. The Department of Education, which oversees Pell Grants, needs to streamline the process postsecondary institutions follow to offer Pell Grant qualified curriculum. Additionally, a strategic and collaborative approach much be taken to bring correctional institutions and colleges together to create a robust post-secondary system that will pay economic dividends for decades to come.

8. **Support Comprehensive Reentry Services**:
The transition from incarceration to stable employment represents a complex societal challenge—not because justice-impacted individuals lack skills or motivation, but because they face interconnected barriers that few are equipped to overcome alone. Many JIPs experience housing instability upon release, lack health insurance, and over 40% live with mental health disorders.[21] These are not isolated issues; they form a domino effect where unstable housing leads to missed job interviews, lack of transportation prevent work consistency and untreated health conditions undermine work performance.

Successful workforce reintegration for justice-impacted individuals requires addressing interconnected barriers through coordinated policy solutions. Creating Medicaid Reentry Waivers that authorize states to use healthcare funds for critical transition services, including pre-release care coordination, substance treatment, and post-release community health support would break the cycle where untreated health issues undermine employment stability. Additionally, Job-Housing Partnerships between the Department of Labor and Department of Housing and Urban Development would combine workforce development with housing security through vouchers tied to employment participation, recognizing that stable housing enables consistent work attendance.

By aligning healthcare, housing, and workforce systems through targeted funding and specialized coordination, we can create sustainable pathways to economic stability that do not just improve individual outcomes—they deliver measurable returns for employers and taxpayers alike.

Measuring Impact & Success

Currently, no standardized metrics exist to evaluate the success of hiring initiatives for justice-impacted people. Without consistent measurement of critical outcomes—including recidivism rates, job retention, and wage growth—progress is stifled. This glaring data gap makes it difficult to compare outcomes across initiatives, optimize successful models, or identify interventions that fail to deliver results. Quantitative data is paramount in assessing program effectiveness, informing policy decisions, and demonstrating the value of workforce integration. When stakeholders—including policymakers, employers, and advocacy groups—have access to reliable metrics, they can replicate best practices, allocate resources strategically, and scale programs that reduce recidivism and improve employment outcomes.

Beyond improving programs, robust measurement transforms perceptions by converting abstract arguments into concrete business cases. Objective data on superior retention rates and productivity levels among JIP employees does more than any advocacy campaign to overcome biases. This evidentiary approach turns skepticism into support, creating a ripple effect that encourages broader adoption of inclusive hiring practices.

The following proposed metrics are designed to establish uniform standards needed to effectively measure the impact of JIP hiring initiatives:

1. **Participation Rate:**
   The percentage of eligible inmates participating in a particular program, training, or initiative.

2. **Graduation Rate**:
   The percentage of participants that graduated from a particular program, training, or initiative.

3. **Post-Release Employment Rate (W-2)**:
   Percentage of JIPs within a cohort that secures employment on a W-2 basis within six months after release from incarceration.

4. **Post-Release Employment Rate (1099)**:

Percentage of JIPs within a cohort that secures employment on a 1099 basis within six months after release from incarceration.

5. **Job Retention Rate (W-2):**
   The percentage of JIPs within a cohort who remain employed at the same company for twelve consecutive months.

6. **Long-Term Post-Release Employment Rate (W-2)**: Percentage of JIPs within a cohort employed on a W-2 basis at the one-year anniversary of their release.

7. **Recidivism Rate (One Year, Three Years, Five Years):** Percentage of JIPs that are charged with a crime within one-year, three-year, and five-year periods. Compare the recidivism rate between JIPs participating in employment training to those that did not.

8. **Employee Dismissal Rate (6 months, 12 months):** Percentage of JIPs dismissed from the role for performance issues at the six month and 12-month hiring anniversary.

9. **Employer Satisfaction Rate (6 months, 12 months):** Issue a survey to the employer at the six-month and 12-month hiring anniversary in line with the Society Human Resource Management (SHRM) standards to gauge satisfaction and employee performance.

10. **Direct Cost Savings Calculation (one year, three years, five years):**

Take the total number of non-program graduates that recidivate minus total number of program graduates that recidivate multiplied by average incarceration cost per individual minus total program cost. Direct Cost Savings Calculation = ((NPG – PG) * Avg Annual Incr. Cost) – Annual Prgm Cost

11. **Total Cost Savings Calculation (one year, three years, five years):**

    Calculate the total cost of the criminal justice system—prosecution, incarceration, social welfare, and lost tax revenue. Then take the total number of non-program graduates that recidivate minus total number of program graduates that recidivate multiplied by average total cost per individual minus total program cost. Total Cost Savings Calculation = ((NPG – PG) * Avg Total Cost) – Annual Prgm Cost

Implementing standardized metrics across the ecosystem will transform success and drive progress. By tracking these outcomes, stakeholders can build compelling, data-driven arguments for the continued support and expansion of these programs. This data infrastructure does more than evaluate performance—it creates a powerful feedback loop that continuously improves reintegration efforts. Ultimately, these metrics serve as both compass and catalyst—guiding policies that reduce recidivism while unlocking economic potential and accelerating prosperity for all.

The systemic employment barriers facing justice-impacted individuals conceal one of America's most overlooked economic opportunities. The current system—marked by fragmented policies, occupational licensing barriers, and inconsistent metrics—stifles employment and perpetuates cycles of recidivism. The United States squanders human potential while incurring avoidable costs—from the approximately $300,000 a year to investigate, prosecute and incarcerate an individual to lost GDP from excluded workers. Yet the path forward is clear. New policy frameworks—from automatic expungement to a streamlined Work Opportunity Tax Credit—offer a blueprint for transforming rehabilitation into economic contribution. The data demonstrates what is possible when systems align with evidence rather than stigma.

Progress demands deviation from the norm. That deviation starts with recognizing justice-impacted individuals not as risks to mitigate, but as talent to cultivate—a workforce segment whose successful integration will define the next era of economic growth and public safety. The data leaves no doubt that when we remove arbitrary barriers and measure what matters, everyone profits.

GUIDE FOR IMPLEMENTING SECOND CHANCE HIRING

"Vision without execution is hallucination."
—Thomas Edison, American inventor and businessman

For businesses seeking to address workforce shortages while making a measurable social impact, implementing second chance hiring requires more than good intentions—it demands a structured operational approach. Developing a step-by-step framework that addresses several key areas including recruitment strategy adjustments, interview process modifications, onboarding enhancements, and retention support is critical to achieve successful outcomes.

By following a strategic roadmap and tactical playbook, companies can access an underutilized talent pool while improving corporate profitability. Additionally, the framework addresses critical implementation factors including policy alignment with organizational objectives and partnership development with reentry organizations. The methodology demonstrates how workforce development goals can align with talent acquisition strategies in today's competitive labor market.

First: Develop & Disseminate the Strategy

Creating a second chance hiring strategy for JIPs involves a structured and thoughtful approach that spans the entire process—recruitment, interviewing, hiring, training, and retention; and crosses the entire organization—human resources, legal, finance, and marketing teams. The first step for a company is to clearly define how second chance hiring aligns with its broader business goals, such as reducing turnover, improving customer lifetime value, or fostering a more inclusive corporate culture. By incorporating team leaders from across the organization early in the process, a business leader can receive feedback, cultivate broad buy-in, and strategize on an effective initial roll-out.

Regarding specific departments, each team leader needs to document the various considerations for hiring, training, and retaining JIPs. This should include developing tailored interview questions, supplemental training procedures, and ongoing mentoring. Once the second chance hiring strategy is developed, the next critical phase is the dissemination and implementation phases. This involves not only rolling out the initiative across the organization but also establishing monitoring, feedback, and adjustment mechanisms.

Marketing should be engaged at an early stage to develop an internal marketing campaign to educate all employees about the second chance hiring initiative. This should include case studies from other companies, key statistics supporting the strategy, and regular updates via newsletters. Simultaneously, marketing teams should lay the foundation and build relationships with media outlets that focus on restorative justice to leverage press releases, interviews, and guest articles in the future. These efforts enhance internal buy-in and position the company externally as a leader in social responsibility.

Implementation should be phased and deliberate, starting with pilot programs in specific departments or regions before scaling up to the entire organization. This phased approach identifies and resolves potential challenges in a controlled environment, ensuring smoother implementation when scaled up across the company. During this phase, training is essential for employees, particularly those in hiring and supervisory roles to ensure they understand the objectives and procedures of the second chance hiring strategy. This training should emphasize the importance of empathy during an onboarding phase and the value JIPs can bring to the organization.

Second: Recruiting & Interviewing

From a process standpoint, the human resources (HR) team should review job postings and the application processes to ensure they do not inadvertently exclude JIPs. For example, many job applications include questions about criminal history that discourage JIPs from applying. Adopting "Ban the Box" policies, which remove the criminal history question from initial job applications, should be a starting point.

However, to effectively recruit JIPs, businesses should establish partnerships with organizations specializing in reentry and workforce development for justice-impacted individuals. These organizations can provide access to a pool of candidates who have undergone extensive skills training and are ready for employment. Businesses can leverage the organization's experience, gain access to high-quality talent, and receive support and guidance in the recruitment process.

Once applications are received, a fair and objective screening process must be implemented that evaluates candidates based on aptitudes, qualifications, and potential rather than their prior experience, background, or formal education. During the interview process, it will be necessary to engage in open and honest conversations with candidates about their criminal history. This can be done in a way that is respectful and non-judgmental, allowing candidates to explain their past and demonstrate how they have rehabilitated and prepared themselves for reentry into the workforce. HR teams and interviewers should be trained to handle these conversations empathetically and professionally, focusing on the candidate's qualifications and readiness to contribute to the organization.

Third: Hiring

When extending a job offer to a justice-impacted individual, it may be appropriate to extend a conditional job offer that outlines specific steps the candidate must complete before finalizing employment. These steps should include running a background check to confirm that the information reported matches the candidate's narrative as well as conducting reference checks with the reentry program to verify completion of programming and/or participation in targeted training programs. By setting these clear conditions, employers can establish transparent expectations and provide a structured path for JIPs to succeed.

Human Resource teams must be trained in individualized background check assessments and collaborate with candidates when inconsistencies are found. A 2013 report from the National Employment Law Project found that nearly half of FBI background checks failed to include information on the outcome of a case after an arrest—such as if a charge was dismissed or a record expunged.[1] Another study in the Journal of Criminology found that more than half of criminal records contained at least one false-positive error, and 90% of records had at least one false-negative error.[2] As a result, background checks should be used to verify the candidate's information instead of as a filtering function. This individualized assessment allows a deeper understanding of each candidate's circumstances and potential.

The finance and legal team should be involved to ensure employers take advantage of incentives designed to encourage hiring JIPs. The Work Opportunity Tax Credit (WOTC) provides federal tax incentives to employers who hire individuals from targeted groups, including JIPs. Additionally, the Federal Bonding Program offers free insurance to employers to protect against the potential risks associated with hiring JIPs.

Fourth: Training & Mentoring

Effective onboarding and training are essential for the success of JIPs in the workplace. Traditional onboarding programs often fail to address the unique challenges JIPs face, such as adapting to a structured work environment after incarceration. To ensure a smooth transition, businesses should implement tailored onboarding initiatives that provide targeted support during the critical early stages of employment. This might include extended orientation sessions, one-on-one meetings with HR, and clear communication of company policies and expectations.

In addition to job-specific training, the onboarding process should emphasize developing soft skills such as mirroring company communication styles and teamwork expectations—skills crucial for thriving in any work environment. This level of tailored support helps JIPs acclimate to their new roles more smoothly and lays the foundation for long-term success and integration into the company culture.

Implementing a formal mentorship program is another critical component to ensure JIPs succeed in the workplace. Pairing JIPs with experienced mentors who can provide guidance, support, and advice is invaluable as these individuals navigate the challenges of reentering the workforce. Mentors are crucial in helping JIPs build confidence, understand workplace dynamics, and develop a sense of belonging within the organization. A well-structured mentorship program not only aids in the professional development of JIPs but also fosters a culture of inclusion and support within the company. This, in turn, can lead to higher job satisfaction, improved retention rates, and increased productivity among all employees as they feel more connected to their roles and the organization.

Fifth: Monitoring & Measuring Impact

To ensure the ongoing success of a second chance hiring strategy, businesses must continuously monitor and adjust the program. HR should establish check-ins on a set cadence to assess the progress of JIPs and address any challenges they may face. These interactions provide an opportunity to offer constructive feedback, celebrate achievements, and ensure that JIPs feel supported and contribute to their roles. In addition, businesses should provide JIPs, and all employees, access to Employee Assistance Programs (EAPs), which offer resources for mental health, financial counseling, and other personal issues that may impact job performance.

The long-term success of a business, its employees, and its strategies depends on accurately measuring the impact of their efforts. Managers and HR teams must closely track key performance indicators, performance ratings, employee satisfaction, and retention rates. Collecting and analyzing this data allows organizations to identify trends, pinpoint areas for improvement, and refine their approaches to better meet the needs of both the JIPs and the company. Regularly assessing the effectiveness of the second chance hiring strategy ensures that it remains dynamic and responsive, ultimately leading to more successful outcomes for JIPs and a more resilient, and productive workforce for the organization.

Sixth: Marketing

Six months after hiring the first JIP—or cohort of JIPs—a business should have enough qualitative and quantitative data to gauge the pilot program's success. Assuming the pilot shows promise, the next step would be to share the impact internally and externally. A business should leverage the partnerships built with NGOs specializing in reentry work. Collaborating with these organizations not only enhances the credibility of your initiative but also extends its reach. Launch joint awareness campaigns with these NGOs to highlight the societal and economic benefits of second chance hiring while demonstrating a business's strong commitment to social responsibility. These campaigns can take various forms, such as public events, webinars, or social media campaigns, all aimed at educating the public and encouraging other businesses to adopt similar practices.

In addition to partnering with NGOs, issuing press releases is a critical component of the marketing strategy. Regularly announcing new initiatives, partnerships, and success stories through press releases helps to maintain momentum and keep the public informed about the company's efforts. These press releases should detail the programs and highlight their impact by including data and testimonials showcasing the positive outcomes for both the company and the community. By distributing these press releases across multiple channels—including local and national media outlets, industry publications, and social media platforms—businesses can maximize their utility.

Marketing to employees is just as important as external communications. Educating employees about the second chance hiring program through internal communication channels helps build a culture of inclusivity, leading to higher job satisfaction and overall retention rates.[3] This can be achieved through campaigns that outline the program's benefits and the roles employees play in supporting it. Sharing success stories of JIPs who have thrived within the company is particularly effective in humanizing the initiative and demonstrating its tangible benefits. These stories can be featured in internal newsletters, highlighted during town hall meetings, or discussed within employee resource groups. By fostering an internal culture that embraces second chance hiring, a business enhances employee engagement and reduces turnover, translating into financial gains.

Business Checklist

For businesses and HR teams, this checklist provides an easy-to-use framework to integrate JIPs into the workforce effectively:

1. **Recruitment**

   Build Awareness: Train staff to understand the benefits of hiring JIPs and address biases.

   Remove Barriers: Adopt "Ban the Box" policies and revise job postings to avoid prefiltering JIPs.

Partner with Reentry Organizations: Collaborate with reentry programs like PEP and Defy Ventures to access qualified candidates.

2. Review

Fair Screening Process: Delay background checks until later stages and make personalized assessments considering the nature of the offense, the time elapsed since the conviction, and evidence of rehabilitation.

Conduct Empathetic Interviews: Engage in respectful discussions about criminal history, focusing on skills, qualifications, and potential.

3. Hiring

Conditional Offers: Provide job offers contingent on confirming criminal history or additional training.

Leverage Incentives: Utilize the Work Opportunity Tax Credit (WOTC) and Federal Bonding Program to reduce hiring risks.

4. Training

Tailored Onboarding: Develop specific onboarding programs for JIPs, including soft skills and technical training.

Mentorship Programs: Pair JIPs with experienced employees to support their transition and development.

5. Retention

Highlight Wins: Promote the second chance initiative and individual success stories through employee resource groups, and internal communication channels.

Continuous Support: Perform regular check-ins, provide access to Employee Assistance Programs (EAPs), and offer professional development opportunities.

Monitor and Adjust: Track key metrics (performance, retention, etc.) and adjust strategies based on data.

6. **Marketing**

   Partner with NGOs: Collaborate with reputable NGOs and launch joint campaigns to bolster credibility and the benefits of second chance hiring.

   Market Externally: Issue press releases to announce initiatives, highlight their impact and leverage various media channels to improve organic visibility through earned media.

   Market Internally: Educate employees through newsletters, town hall meetings, or resource groups about the second chance hiring program. Share success stories and explain how they can support long-term business performance.

This checklist ensures that businesses, regardless of industry or size, develop a comprehensive and effective strategy for hiring and retaining JIPs, fostering both organizational success and social impact.

CHAPTER 9

LEVERAGING TECHNOLOGY IN REENTRY

"Failure is not fatal, but failure to change might be."
—John Wooden, Hall of Fame UCLA Basketball coach

Emerging technologies have the potential to transform how justice-impacted people prepare for and transition into the workforce. Innovative tools—from AI-driven education platforms to virtual reality skills training—can effectively bridge the gap between incarceration and employment. These solutions not only address traditional reentry barriers but also align with the evolving demands of the modern labor market.

For governmental organizations, reentry programs, and employers exploring second chance hiring, these technological advancements present practical opportunities. From remote monitoring technologies to virtual mentorship networks, embracing innovation can reduce costs while ensuring accountability. Data shows that when implemented effectively, such tools enhance both individual outcomes and systemic efficiency.

As workforce needs shift and technology continues to advance, these innovations will become increasingly vital to successful reintegration. The benefits extend across the ecosystem—empowering government officials managing cases, equipping employers with untapped talent, and supporting individuals as they rebuild their lives.

Educational Technologies

Artificial Intelligence (AI) is in the early stages of revolutionizing industries by automating processes and creating demand for new skills and jobs. Equipping JIPs with AI proficiency—particularly in tools like ChatGPT—opens doors to a growing sector that prioritizes digital literacy, problem-solving, and innovation.

AI tools like ChatGPT offer JIPs a powerful way to develop essential communication skills. These platforms can simulate real-world workplace interactions, deliver instant feedback, and allow for unlimited practice—helping users refine their professionalism, tone, and clarity. For JIPs reentering society after incarceration, this is especially valuable. AI bridges gaps in communication experience, enabling JIPs to rebuild confidence and fluency in a judgment-free environment. As they sharpen communication skills, they become better prepared for job interviews, team collaboration, and workplace integration—key factors in securing and sustaining employment.

Online learning platforms will be the next frontier of the AI revolution, transforming education by delivering flexible, personalized instruction tailored to each student's needs. Platforms like Coursera, edX, and Khan Academy are beginning to leverage AI to analyze a student's progress in real time, dynamically adjusting content difficulty to keep them engaged and challenged but not overwhelmed. This adaptability is especially valuable for JIPs who often need to balance education with other reentry challenges.

Online learning platforms also offer the flexibility needed to accommodate unique schedules, allowing JIPs to learn asynchronously at their own pace, making it easier to integrate education into their reentry process. Additionally, these learning platforms can be offered on tablets, which are now available to over one million individuals in prison.[1] Several studies have revealed a moderate beneficial effect of using mobile devices in education compared to using desktop computers, making tablets an ideal tool for delivering scalable, effective training.[2] The technological innovation in eLearning—whether by desktop or tablet—represents a powerful tool for overcoming barriers to education, offering a pathway to skill development and employment specialization.

Virtual Reality (VR) is emerging as a game-changing tool for workforce development, offering immersive, hands-on training in high-demand fields. Through VR simulations, JIPs can gain practical experience in skilled trades—such as aircraft maintenance, construction, or drilling operations—within a safe, controlled environment. Unlike traditional training, VR drastically reduces costs while allowing trainees to practice complex tasks repeatedly until mastery. This technology not only accelerates skill acquisition but also builds confidence, preparing JIPs for real-world job challenges before they even step onto a worksite.

Tesla faces a critical bottleneck as its 5-million-strong vehicle fleet ages: a severe shortage of technicians qualified to service its advanced battery systems that wear out over time, requiring repair or replacement.[3] With a shortage of specialized technicians capable of handling the battery maintenance, these electric vehicles (EVs) risk becoming a consumable technology, like a TV that gets discarded after 5 to 10 years of use—undermining both sustainability goals and consumer trust in the brand.[4]

An innovative solution lies in cultivating a new workforce comprised of JIPs trained through a comprehensive two-phase program. First, participants would master EV battery fundamentals through a six-month online learning platform like Coursera. Next, they would undergo up to twelve months of immersive VR training, gaining experience through realistic simulations of battery diagnostics and repairs—from cell degradation analysis to module replacement. Graduates would emerge as certified technicians, ready to fill Tesla's urgent labor gap upon reentry. This initiative would transform a business challenge into a strategic advantage as Tesla gains a scalable, skilled workforce to maintain its expanding fleet; consumers benefit from extended vehicle lifespans; and JIPs secure a direct pathway to high-demand careers in the new economy. The program would not just solve a logistical problem—it would improve Tesla's financials and reinforce the company's leadership in both technological and operational innovation.

Cutting-edge educational technologies—from AI-driven learning platforms to immersive VR training—hold immense potential to empower JIPs with workforce-ready skills. When integrated into reentry programs, these tools do more than teach technical competencies; they rebuild confidence, bridge opportunity gaps, and create pathways to meaningful employment. The data supporting these technologies is compelling, showing improved learning outcomes, increased engagement, and greater skills specialization, which benefits participants, companies, and society. By investing in these scalable solutions, we can transform systemic barriers into launchpads for success.

Improved Job Matching & Placement

Conventional job-seeking methods frequently disadvantage JIPs, who often lack professional networks and face systemic biases in hiring. Digital platforms can revolutionize this process by using intelligent matching algorithms to connect JIPs' skills with employer needs—eliminating traditional gatekeepers. Virtual career fairs further democratize access, allowing JIPs to showcase their qualifications to multiple employers simultaneously from any location. These tech-driven solutions create new pathways to economic mobility that bypass traditional barriers to employment.

Online job portals have revolutionized the job search process by offering a centralized platform where JIPs can access a wide range of employment opportunities tailored to their needs and circumstances. Realizing the opportunity to service this large market, the job site Indeed now employs sophisticated AI algorithms to analyze skills, experience, and preferences, enabling precise job matches for JIPs. By using AI to analyze vast amounts of data, Indeed identifies patterns and preferences leading to more accurate job matches, ultimately increasing the chances of successful employment for JIPs.[5] Meanwhile, specialized platforms such as Honest Jobs have emerged to directly connect JIPs with employers committed to fair-chance hiring. Research from the Urban Institute shows that JIPs using these tailored platforms are 30% more likely to secure employment within six months of release compared to those relying on conventional methods.[6] By democratizing access to opportunity and reducing unconscious bias through data-driven matching, these digital solutions are transforming hiring challenges into workforce victories.

Traditional resume screening often overlooks candidates with non-linear career paths or gaps in employment, which are common among JIPs. However, advancements in AI algorithms help overcome these barriers by focusing on skill-based matching rather than solely on work history. SkillSmart has pioneered an innovative approach that matches candidates to jobs based on specific skills required by employers. SkillSmart's system breaks down job descriptions into their core competencies and then matches these with the skills listed in a candidate's profile—a JIP with experience in carpentry gained through a prison vocational program could be matched with construction companies looking for those precise skills, even if the candidate lacks formal job experience in the industry.[7] The impact of skill-matching technologies is significant. A report by Harvard Business Review found that companies using AI-based skill-matching technologies saw a 20% increase in the diversity of their candidate pool, including the hiring of more individuals with non-traditional backgrounds, such as JIPs.[8]

Given that JIPs often face mobility constraints—such as unreliable transportation or probation restrictions—virtual career fairs provide a crucial opportunity to connect with employers, attend workshops, and interview from anywhere. Data from Glassdoor indicates that companies participating in virtual career fairs report a 35% higher engagement rate from diverse candidates, including those from marginalized groups such as JIPs, compared to traditional in-person job fairs.[9] Another study by Indeed found that candidates who participated in virtual career fairs were 40% more likely to secure a job interview compared to those who did not, highlighting the importance of these platforms in the modern job search process.[10] This digital approach particularly benefits JIPs by enabling them to simultaneously connect with multiple employers, develop professional skills through virtual workshops, and interview for positions—effectively compressing what would normally require weeks of travel and scheduling into convenient remote connections. By removing geographical and logistical hurdles, virtual career fairs are proving to be a valuable solution for connecting overlooked talent with meaningful employment opportunities.

Cutting-edge digital platforms are revolutionizing employment access for justice-impacted individuals by dismantling systemic barriers. Through intelligent job matching algorithms, skills-first hiring technologies, and virtual career fairs, these solutions create unprecedented pathways to economic mobility. Platforms now leverage AI to bypass traditional hiring biases, while virtual career fairs eliminate geographical restrictions—particularly crucial for JIPs facing probation limitations and transportation hurdles. Empirical evidence demonstrates their transformative impact to improve job matching precision, expand professional networks, and significantly increase employment rates post-release. As these technologies continue advancing, they are facilitating individual success stories and actively reshaping labor markets to value potential over pedigree, creating a more equitable future of work where an individual's skills matter more than their past.

Mentorship & Support Networks

Mentorship is a vital factor to help justice-impacted individuals successfully reintegrate into society. By offering guidance and support, mentors assist JIPs in overcoming the challenges of reentry. Traditional mentorship programs often struggle with limitations such as geographical barriers, shortage of mentors, and scalability challenges.

Digital mentorship programs leverage technology to extend both the reach and impact by connecting JIPs with mentors regardless of location or transportation constraints. Research from the Yale Program for Recovery and Community Health highlights the effectiveness of mentorship, showing that mentees in such programs are more likely to achieve their reentry goals than those without mentorship support.[11]

Peer support is a cornerstone of successful reentry for JIPs. Peer-to-peer platforms create a space where JIPs can connect with others who share similar experiences, offering mutual understanding, encouragement, and practical guidance. These platforms help combat isolation and stigma by fostering a sense of community—a crucial factor for individuals rebuilding their lives post-incarceration. With features like forums, chat rooms, and video conferencing, participants can engage in real-time or asynchronous discussions, ensuring accessibility and flexibility. AI algorithms further enhance these platforms by analyzing user profiles and behavior to facilitate meaningful, supportive connections. A report by the Center for Public Policy Priorities found that JIPs who participated in peer support programs had a 69% lower recidivism rate after three years compared to those without such support.[12]

When used constructively, social media and online community groups can serve as powerful tools to aid in the reintegration of JIPs. By joining reentry-focused groups, JIPs can share their experiences and seek advice with others who understand their challenges. These digital spaces are especially valuable for those without reliable in-person support systems or access to formalized mentorship programs. Facebook, Reddit, Skool, and other specialized forums allow JIPs to exchange job leads, educational opportunities, and firsthand insights. AI can enhance these communities by filtering harmful content, recommending relevant connections, and ensuring productive interactions. When used intentionally, social media transforms into a lifeline—helping JIPs rebuild their lives through shared knowledge and collective support.

Digital mentorship programs, peer-to-peer platforms, and online support groups provide scalable, accessible solutions that expand critical support for JIPs. Enhanced by AI-driven tools, these platforms deliver personalized guidance and 24/7 assistance, creating meaningful connections that empower JIPs to overcome reentry challenges and build brighter futures.

Monitoring & Management Tools for Reintegration

The U.S. government's current monitoring systems and management tools for JIPs are outdated, costly, and counterproductive. These antiquated probation, parole, and home confinement technologies create unnecessary financial burdens for all parties while imposing unnecessary barriers on individuals seeking to rebuild their lives.

Outdated supervision methods subject JIPs to intrusive and counterproductive demands—from disruptive 24/7 verification calls to unexpected mandatory in-person check-ins that jeopardize employment stability. These inefficient practices waste government resources while actively undermining successful reintegration, despite the availability of more effective remote monitoring solutions. Recent advances in technology have revolutionized supervision capabilities, introducing powerful tools like facial recognition software, computer vision cameras, pinpoint global positioning satellite (GPS) monitoring, transdermal alcohol sensors, and wearable drug detection devices. These innovative solutions provide unprecedented convenience and accountability through real-time monitoring—ensuring compliance while dramatically reducing costs and improving outcomes for JIPs.

GPS trackers, also known as electronic monitoring devices (EMD), are the primary supervision tool for individuals across all phases—pretrial, home confinement, and probation. Although the headline costs are high in certain jurisdictions, EMDs have proven to be a successful and cost-effective way to monitor individuals in comparison to incarceration. A study by the University of Ontario Institute of Technology found individuals with EMD supervision had an 8.17% failure-to-appear rate compared to 22.59% for non-monitored individual—a 64% decrease in failure rate.[13] A second study from the Department of Justice showed that GPS monitoring reduces supervision failures by 31%.[14] The financial advantages are equally compelling with 2022 U.S. Federal Courts data showing that EMDs cost taxpayers a mere $4 per day ($1,460 annually), compared with $101 a day for pretrial detention ($36,865 annually), and $123 a day for post-conviction imprisonment ($44,895 annually)—a 96% reduction in costs. These findings collectively establish EMD technology as an operationally effective and fiscally responsible supervision solution that enhances compliance while dramatically reducing taxpayer burdens.

Despite EMDs proven effectiveness and cost savings, persistent misconceptions remain about technological limitations and potential for substance abuse violations during home confinement. This has led many prosecutors and judges to view incarceration as the only reliable form of punishment. However, next-generation monitoring solutions—including facial recognition software, computer vision enabled cameras, transdermal alcohol sensors, and advanced wearables—now address these concerns directly. By providing comprehensive, real-time oversight, these innovations can shift judicial attitudes toward probation and home confinement sentences. This transition maintains public safety while also preserving workforce participation and economic productivity that would otherwise be lost to incarceration.

Advanced facial recognition and computer vision technologies now enable comprehensive remote monitoring that goes beyond simple location verification. These systems can detect potential intoxication through AI-powered analysis of speech patterns, eye movements, and facial coloration. The process begins with an in-person baseline assessment, where an individual reads a standardized script to establish their sober profile. Subsequent remote check-ins require on-demand video recordings that are instantly analyzed for signs of impairment—from speech irregularities to flushed cheeks. When integrated with transdermal alcohol sensors and drug-detecting wearables, these solutions create a robust, real-time monitoring ecosystem. Case managers can receive immediate alerts for potential violations, enabling prompt intervention while dramatically reducing the need for in-person check-ins. This technological approach presents a triple win by decreasing reliance on costly incarceration, minimizing burdensome manual supervision, and improving outcomes for justice-impacted individuals—all while saving billions for taxpayers.

Parole officers, social workers, and other reintegration professionals currently struggle with outdated case management systems that create operational inefficiencies, resource misallocation, and unnecessary public safety risks. Modern solutions must consolidate critical data—employment, housing, health, finances, and compliance—while incorporating predictive analytics to identify emerging risks before they escalate.

The government and reentry organizations could leverage existing project management platforms like Monday.com or ClickUp—tools already proven effective in complex organizational settings—to streamline case monitoring. These systems offer customizable dashboards, automated reminders, and real-time collaboration features that could dramatically improve case management efficiency while reducing administrative burdens.

Beyond individual case oversight, aggregated analytics can reveal systemic patterns, empowering data-driven policy decisions. The Council of State Governments Justice Center demonstrated this potential, achieving a 23% reduction in reincarceration rates since 2008 through analytic informed program improvements.[15]

We stand at a pivotal moment where emerging technologies can revolutionize JIP sentencing and supervision. Integrating advanced monitoring systems with intelligent case management platforms presents an unprecedented opportunity to reduce unnecessary incarceration and improve rehabilitation outcomes while delivering significant cost savings for taxpayers. By replacing archaic manual practices with AI-powered tools we can reduce recidivism, preserve employment stability, and optimize limited resources. These solutions offer a balanced approach—enhancing accountability without sacrificing reintegration success—proving that innovation and justice need not be mutually exclusive. The path forward requires embracing technology to build a system that prioritizes both public safety and human potential.

CHAPTER 10

AN ECONOMIC IMPERATIVE

"Pessimists sound smart. Optimists make money."
—Nat Friedman CEO Github

Forward-thinking executives and policymakers are awakening to the proven economic value of second chance hiring. Beyond its social merits, employing justice-impacted individuals delivers measurable financial returns that strengthen both organizational performance and economic growth.

For business executives, this approach yields distinct competitive advantages by reducing turnover costs, increasing productivity, and strengthening brand reputation. For policymakers, reducing employment barriers alleviates labor shortages spurring economic activity while reducing related public expenditures—creating a fiscal win-win for communities.

By utilizing data-driven approaches and an evidence based framework, the United States can achieve concrete economic advantages of second chance hiring without sacrificing social safety. When implemented strategically, hiring justice-impacted individuals becomes undeniable business and economic imperative.

For Executives: Improve Long-Term Financials

In an era of fierce competition, adopting innovative and sustainable practices is more pressing than ever. Companies need to continuously improve their financials, not just through conventional cost-cutting measures but by exploring untapped resources that can drive both profitability and organizational efficiencies—employing justice-impacted individuals is one such opportunity. This approach is not a moral imperative but a financially sound decision that can bring significant economic benefits to company and country. By hiring JIPs, businesses can unlock a myriad of direct benefits—a reduction in operational costs, an increase in productivity, enhanced employee loyalty, and higher customer satisfaction—all of which ultimately drive higher revenue and profit margins.

Reduction in Turnover Costs

One of the most significant financial benefits of hiring JIPs is reducing turnover costs. Employees with a criminal background often exhibit a higher loyalty and commitment to their employers, which translates into lower turnover rates. Companies like Total Wine & More and Electronic Recyclers International (ERI) report a reduction in turnover in the range of 10% up to 50%. Evidence shows that JIPs tend to stay longer in their roles due to the value they place on the opportunity for stable employment, leading to a more consistent and reliable workforce. Considering that the cost to replace an employee can range from 50%-200% of an employee's annual salary, these reductions in turnover result in material cost savings over time, not only through decreased hiring expenses but also by preserving institutional knowledge and thereby increasing productivity levels.

Increased Productivity

Beyond a reduction in turnover, JIPs frequently demonstrate an exceptional drive and work ethic that directly benefit businesses. Having overcome substantial employment barriers, these workers often display remarkable commitment to excelling in their roles. This translates into measurable productivity gains—from volunteering for extra tasks to delivering meticulous work quality. Industry leaders like Dave's Killer Bread and Televerde consistently observe their justice-impacted staff surpass performance benchmarks, fueled by a deep sense of purpose and determination to succeed.

These employees also contribute unique viewpoints shaped by diverse life experiences, fostering creative problem-solving and fresh approaches to challenges. Their distinct perspectives frequently spark process improvements and innovative ideas that elevate entire teams. Together, these qualities create a powerful productivity multiplier at the individual, team, and company level. The combination of these factors creates a sustained competitive advantage in the marketplace.

Government Incentives

For business leaders, hiring JIPs can unlock significant government incentives. Through programs like the Work Opportunity Tax Credit (WOTC), companies can claim up to $9,600 in tax credit for each qualified hire—a credit that directly reduces a company's tax liability, effectively turning hiring JIPs into a cost-saving initiative.

The Federal Bonding Program further incentivizes hiring justice-impacted individuals by providing employers with *free* fidelity insurance for the first six months of employment—covering up to $25,000 in potential theft or dishonesty losses. This initiative directly addresses employer concerns about risk, effectively removing a major barrier to second chance hiring. With a degree of financial protection in place, businesses can confidently tap into this motivated talent pool while mitigating perceived liabilities.

Companies that adopt second chance hiring gain access to exclusive grant funding from government agencies and nonprofit organizations dedicated to workforce development. These financial resources—often overlooked by competitors—can subsidize job training, mentorship programs, and employee support services specifically designed for justice-impacted hires. This strategic advantage allows businesses to build a pipeline of skilled workers while redirecting would-be training budgets to other critical operations, creating a self-reinforcing cycle of talent development and cost optimization.

Enhanced Organizational Culture

Second chance hiring transforms workplace culture into a powerful competitive advantage. By championing redemption and inclusion, companies unlock higher employee engagement, stronger team cohesion, and measurable performance gains—all while positioning themselves as employers of choice in today's values-driven talent market.

This commitment to social impact resonates deeply with modern workers. Organizations that prioritize people over past mistakes cultivate uncommon levels of trust and loyalty, creating workplaces where employees feel genuinely valued. The ripple effects are far-reaching—teams become more innovative as diverse life experiences spark creative problem-solving, and top performers gravitate toward corporate cultures that exhibit authenticity and psychological safety. In today's competitive job market, high-performing individuals are not just looking for a paycheck—they seek out companies that align with their values. This enhances the company's competitive edge and fosters a culture of innovation and collaboration, as diverse perspectives are more likely to drive creative solutions and ideas.

Strategic Marketing Advantage

Hiring JIPs offers a strategic advantage beyond social responsibility—it creates measurable brand value in today's purpose-driven marketplace. Companies that lead with second chance initiatives unlock a powerful PR advantage, earning organic media coverage, influencer endorsements, and consumer goodwill that traditional advertising cannot match. This strategic visibility positions brands as authentic social innovators while forging deeper connections with the consumers. By transforming HR policies into compelling brand narratives, companies turn what was once thought of as social responsibility into a competitive edge that drives both brand loyalty and revenue.

Improved Brand Loyalty

In today's marketplace, consumers actively seek out brands that align with their values—and few initiatives resonate as powerfully as second chance hiring. Companies that implement these practices do not just check a CSR box, they position themselves as authentic leaders in social justice, earning deeper customer loyalty and attracting new demographics. Research consistently shows that purpose-driven consumers—who now represent the majority—will choose, pay more for, and remain loyal to brands making tangible social impacts. This alignment leads to increased customer retention and higher lifetime customer value.

The benefits multiply through organic marketing with positive media coverage, viral social sharing, and word-of-mouth advocacy from customers who become genuine brand ambassadors. This creates a virtuous cycle where social responsibility fuels reputation, which in turn drives financial performance—transforming ethical hiring practices into both immediate PR wins and sustainable competitive advantage.

Revenue Growth

Second chance hiring delivers powerful market differentiation that directly fuels revenue growth. By embracing this approach, companies boost brand awareness and attract a growing customer base that values social responsibility. Research confirms consumers are willing to pay premium prices for products from socially responsible companies, allowing businesses to capture new market segments and expand their share among socially conscious buyers.

The benefits extend beyond customer acquisition. Second chance hiring generates positive media coverage and enhances public perception, amplifying marketing effectiveness and driving sales conversions. In today's competitive landscape, where consumers increasingly favor brands demonstrating tangible social impact, strategic implementation of second chance hiring creates a sustainable growth engine. Companies that adopt these practices position themselves for long-term success in an evolving marketplace that rewards both profitability and purpose.

EBITDA Growth

Second chance hiring drives bottom-line results through a unique combination of revenue growth and operational efficiency. By reducing turnover costs, boosting workforce productivity, and leveraging available tax incentives, companies ultimately see improvements to their profit margins. When these savings are reinvested into the business—whether through enhanced employee training, product development, or marketing—they drive further growth and profitability. Additionally, companies with strong CSR commitments enjoy higher customer retention and lifetime value—key drivers of sustainable profitability.

The combination of cost savings, brand loyalty, and improved organizational culture positions companies to achieve significant quantitative and qualitative benefits—second chance hiring is a strategic initiative that can deliver substantial financial returns.

As JIP hiring programs scale and optimize, the flywheel spins faster with positive economic gains compounding, driving sustainable profitability over the long term.

For Politicians: Reduce Taxes & Improve the Economy

Policymakers hold a transformative opportunity to unlock trillions in economic value by prioritizing legislative reforms that empower justice-impacted individuals to join the workforce. Strategic measures that reduce occupational licensing barriers, create targeted tax incentives for employers, and expand evidence-based reentry programs could boost GDP growth rates up to 75% while building a more inclusive economy. This approach activates an underutilized talent pool that can drive national prosperity for decades to come.

Enact Clean Slate Legislation

The lifelong collateral consequences of a criminal record remain one of the most devastating barriers facing justice-impacted individuals, which persists even after rehabilitation and years of law-abiding conduct. Clean slate legislation—which automatically expunges or seals records after a demonstrated period of crime-free living—represents the most effective policy solution to ensure JIPs have a fair opportunity to reintegrate into society and contribute to the economy. By removing artificial barriers to employment, housing, and education, such laws do more than restore individual dignity; they create measurable economic value. Research shows that when people can access stable jobs and housing, recidivism rates plummet while workforce participation and local economies strengthen. This is not merely about second chances—it is about recognizing that continued punishment after completing a sentence serves neither justice nor societal interests. The implementation of clean slate laws offers a rare policy opportunity that simultaneously advances social equity, economic growth, and public safety, making it one of the most consequential reforms for building a more prosperous society.

Reform Occupational Licensing

Outdated occupational licensing laws systematically exclude justice-impacted individuals from meaningful employment—particularly in high-demand fields like healthcare, construction, and education that urgently need skilled workers. Many states maintain counterproductive blanket bans that automatically disqualify applicants with criminal records, regardless of rehabilitation, job qualifications, or time since offense—effectively shutting out individuals from entire industries.

Thoughtful reforms that replace these prohibitions with individualized assessments will open critical job opportunities for JIPs while simultaneously addressing critical labor shortages. This approach appeases all constituents by filling labor shortages for businesses, reducing unemployment for the community, saving resources for taxpayers, all while stimulating economic growth. Modernizing occupational licensing laws is a pragmatic step to strengthen local economies.

Offer Incentives to Businesses

Expanding and streamlining the Work Opportunity Tax Credit (WOTC) presents policymakers with a rare win-win opportunity to cut justice system costs and create safer, more prosperous communities. By enhancing tax incentives for employers who hire justice-impacted individuals—and simplifying the often cumbersome application process—lawmakers can dramatically boost second chance hiring. Steady employment reduces recidivism and dismantles the crushing burden of incarceration, creating a cascade of savings downstream—every dollar spent on incarceration generates an additional $10 in social costs—$1.2 *trillion* in total spending. Meaningful employment breaks the cycle converting crippling hidden costs into productive value.

Strengthening the Federal Bonding Program represents a extraordinary policy win of low risk and high reward. Increasing bond amounts and extending coverage periods, incentivizes businesses to participate in second chance hiring at minimal government cost while delivering measurable community benefits. Given the program's remarkable 1% loss rate, the United States can virtually eliminate employer risk at no cost.

This smart investment yields outsized returns as more justice-impacted individuals gain employment, businesses access an untapped talent pool with zero financial risk, and communities benefit from reduced crime and recidivism. For policymakers, the appeal is undeniable—champion both fiscal responsibility and social progress while delivering concrete results that resonate with voters: safer neighborhoods, stronger local economies, and more efficient use of taxpayer dollars.

Investing in Reentry Services

Investing in reentry services for JIPs is not a moral obligation but an economic necessity. The true cost of recidivism extends far beyond prison walls—each repeat incarceration strains justice systems, drains taxpayer resources, and fractures communities. By strategically funding reentry organizations, the United States unlocks agile solutions tailored to local needs. Local organizations can adapt swiftly to regional job market trends, cultural contexts, and leverage community connections, allowing them to pilot innovative programs, refine approaches in real time, and scale successful initiatives.

By equipping JIPs with market-relevant skills and comprehensive support, their employment prospects soar while recidivism plummets. This dual impact strengthens public safety and generates substantial savings—reducing burdens on law enforcement, social services, and municipal budgets.

Social Impact Bonds

Social Impact Bonds (SIBs) represent a groundbreaking opportunity for policymakers to ignite economic progress while minimizing taxpayer risk. This innovative financing model aligns the interests of investors, government, and service providers by tying financial returns to measurable outcomes. Operating on a performance-based approach, in the SIB model private investors fund evidence-based reentry programs designed to achieve predetermined success metrics—such as reduce recidivism by 20% over two years. This creates a clear accountability mechanism where financial returns are directly tied to measurable social impact. The government only repays investors—typically at a modest return pegged to benchmarks like the Fed Funds Rate + 3%—if the program succeeds, with the added benefit of tax-exempt status similar to municipal bonds. Should a program fall short, the loss is borne by the investors, not taxpayers. By transferring due diligence and risk to the private sector while maintaining accountability for outcomes, SIBs create a win-win scenario of incentivizing high-performing social programs while ensuring public dollars are allocated in a capitalist manner. For policymakers, SIBs offer cost-effective solutions to a complex social challenge and a fiscally responsible path to meaningful impact.

Conclusion: The Economic Imperative

In the dynamic and ever-evolving global economy, businesses and policymakers must continually seek innovative strategies to drive growth, enhance competitiveness, and foster prosperity. One often overlooked strategy holds immense potential, the integration of justice-impacted people into the workforce. As explored throughout this book, employing JIPs is not an act of social responsibility, it is an economic necessity with profound benefits for businesses, governments, and for society at large.

Bridging the Labor and Skills Gap

The United States faces a pressing labor shortage and skills crisis, particularly in critical industries such as technology, healthcare, and construction. Employers struggle to fill these high-demand roles, resulting in lower productivity, project delays, and lost revenue. These persistent workforce gaps highlight the urgent need to explore alternative talent sources—and justice-impacted individuals represent a vast, untapped reservoir of talent.

Through second chance employment initiatives, JIPs can bridge the gap between the segmented labor markets. With targeted training and education, JIPs can develop the skills needed to thrive in today's economy. By investing in their transition into the workforce, businesses gain access to a dedicated and resilient talent pool—driving both organizational success and economic growth.

Reducing Costs and Enhancing Productivity

Employing justice-impacted individuals offers a powerful financial incentive for lower turnover and reduced hiring costs. Research consistently shows that employees with criminal records demonstrate higher retention rates and exhibit strong motivation to excel—largely because they deeply value the opportunity to work and are determined to prove their worth.

Employee turnover represents a substantial financial burden, with replacement costs ranging from 50%-200% of an employee's annual salary. By hiring JIPs—who demonstrate higher retention rates—employers can significantly reduce these expenses. Furthermore, many JIPs possess vocational training acquired during incarceration, decreasing the need for extensive technical onboarding and enabling immediate contributions to organizational productivity.

Companies that adopt second chance hiring practices frequently report measurable gains in productivity. JIPs resilience, determination, and diverse perspectives inspire creativity and enhance team morale. By cultivating a more inclusive workforce, companies enhance their problem-solving capabilities and sharpen their competitive edge in an increasingly fast-moving economy.

Enhancing Brand Image

In today's socially conscious marketplace, corporate social responsibility (CSR) is not just an ethical obligation but a strategic advantage. Consumers are increasingly looking to support companies that demonstrate a commitment to social good, and hiring JIPs is a powerful way for businesses to enhance their CSR profile.

Fostering an inclusive and equitable corporate culture can lead to increased customer loyalty, enhanced brand perception, and, ultimately, higher revenue. Research from Deloitte shows that purpose-driven companies grow three times faster than their peers and see increased stock returns, highlighting the financial benefits of strong CSR initiatives. Additionally, companies known for their inclusive hiring practices often receive positive media attention, attracting top talent and a loyal customer base, providing a competitive edge in an increasingly competitive market.

Reduce Recidivism and Enhance Public Safety

The largest societal benefit of hiring justice-impacted individuals is the substantial reduction in recidivism rates. Stable employment is the critical deterrent to reoffending by providing financial security, meaningful purpose, and social stability. Research consistently shows that employed JIPs are far less likely to return to criminal activity, resulting in safer communities and lower public safety expenditures.

The economic implications of reduced recidivism are undeniable: lower reoffending rates decrease demand for law enforcement interventions, reduce court caseloads, and alleviate overcrowding in correctional facilities—collectively saving billions for taxpayers. These funds can then be reinvested in vital public services like education, healthcare, and infrastructure development.

Furthermore, employed JIPs actively contribute to economic growth through increased consumer spending and tax revenues. This economic participation supports local businesses, funds government programs, and creates a positive cycle of economic growth. By embracing second chance hiring practices, society benefits from both immediate cost reductions in social services and long-term gains from a more productive workforce.

Conclusion: A Call to Action

The integration of justice-impacted individuals into the workforce transcends social responsibility—it represents an economic imperative with transformative potential for businesses, communities, and the national economy. By harnessing this underutilized talent pool through second chance hiring practices, employers and policymakers can simultaneously stimulate growth, reduce costs, and improve public safety.

For business owners, the advantages are compelling: lower turnover and recruitment costs, access to tax incentives, measurable productivity gains, and strengthened corporate reputation. For policymakers, second chance employment initiatives offer a triple benefit—significant taxpayer savings, improved public safety, and broad economic expansion through workforce participation.

The path forward requires concerted action from all stakeholders. Businesses must reform hiring practices while governments invest in education, training, and reintegration programs. By dismantling systemic barriers to employment, the United States can unlock the potential of this vital workforce. The potential is real. The time to act is now—and the rewards will echo across our economy and society for generations to come.

APPENDIX

"Everything feels unprecedented
when you haven't engaged with history."
—Kelly Hayes, American author

Introduction

[1] National Conference of State Legislatures, *Criminal Records and Reentry Toolkit.* March 31, 2023.

[2] Eberstadt, Nicolas, *Statement before the Joint Economic Committee on the Economic Impacts of the 2020 Census and Business Uses of Federal Data: America's Invisible Felon Population: A Blind Spot in U.S. National Statistics.* Henry Wendt Chair in Political Economy, May 22, 2019.

[3] Durose, Matthew R. and Leonardo Antenangeli, *Recidivism of Prisoners Released in 34 States in 2012: A 5-Year Follow-Up Period (2012–2017).* Washington, DC: Bureau of Justice Statistics, 2021.

[4] Craigie, Terry-Ann, Ames Grawert, Cameron Kimble, and Joseph E. Stiglitz, *Conviction, Imprisonment, and Lost Earnings: How Involvement with the Criminal Justice System Deepens Inequality.* Research Report, September 15, 2020.

[5] Award.Co, *Why Worry About Employee Turnover?.* December 4, 2024.

[6] McFeely, Shane and Ben Wigert, *This Fixable Problem Costs U.S. Businesses $1 Trillion.* Gallup.Com, December 12, 2024.

[7] Heinz, Kate, *The True Costs of Employee Turnover.* Built In, July 17, 2024.

[8] Jobvite, *The Real Cost of Employee Turnover (and How to Prevent It).* Jobvite | Recruiting Software - Applicant Tracking (blog), August 14, 2024.

[9] Alper, Mariel, Matthew R. Durose, and Joshua Markman. *2018 Update on Prisoner Recidivism: A 9-Year Follow-Up Period (2005-2014).* Washington, DC: U.S.

Department of Justice, Office of Justice Programs, Bureau of Justice Statistics, 2018.

[10] CSG Justice Center. "Confined and Costly - CSG Justice Center," April 11, 2024.

[11] The Last Mile. *Home - The Last Mile,* November 9, 2024.

[12] Initiative for a Competitive Inner City (ICIC). *Impact Analysis of the Prison Entrepreneurship Program: Reducing Recidivism and Creating Economic Opportunity.* July 2018.

[13] Aos, Steven, and Elizabeth Drake. *Prison, Police, and Programs: Evidence-Based Options That Reduce Crime and Save Money.* Olympia: Washington State Institute for Public Policy, 2013.

[14] CSG Justice Center. "The Cost of Recidivism: - CSG Justice Center," April 26, 2023.

[15] Aslim, Erkmen G., Murat C. Mungan, and Han Yu. "A Welfare Analysis of Medicaid and Recidivism." *Health Economics* 33, 2024.

Chapter 1

[1] Jobvite, *The Real Cost of Employee Turnover (and How to Prevent It).* Jobvite | Recruiting Software - Applicant Tracking (blog), August 14, 2024.

[2] Hayes, Adam, *Labor Force Participation Rate: Purpose, Formula, and Trends.* Investopedia, November 15, 2024.

[3] Ciapponi, Daniel, *The Skills Gap in the Hospitality Industry.* Hospitality Insights, September 4, 2023.

[4] NCSBN, *NCSBN Research Projects Significant Nursing Workforce Shortages and Crisis.* April 13, 2023.

[5] Tappe, Anneken, *Nearly Half of American Companies Say They Are Short on Skilled Workers.* CNN, October 25, 2021.

[6] Hartmann, Anath, *A Second chance in Manufacturing Pays Dividends*. NAM, July 14, 2021.

[7] United Nations, *Leaving No One Behind in an Ageing World (World Social Report 2023)*. 2023.

[8] Cato Institute, *Effects of Immigration on Entrepreneurship and Innovation*. June 18, 2022.

[9] New American Economy, *Entrepreneurship: How Immigration Plays a Critical Role*. September 13, 2015.

[10] OECD, *Migration*. 2024.

[11] SHRM Online Staff, *SHRM Benchmarking Report: $4,129 Average Cost-per-Hire*. SHRM, December 21, 2023.

[12] Deloitte Insights, *2018 Deloitte Skills Gap and Future of Work in Manufacturing Study*. 2018.

[13] MIT Technology Review, *New Approaches to the Tech Talent Shortage*. September 20, 2023.

[14] Diez, Luis M., *The Global Youth Unemployment Rate Is Three Times Greater Than Between Adults*. Youth Employment Decade, January 25, 2018.

[15] Abel, Jaison R. and Richard Deitz, *Job Polarization and Rising Inequality in the Nation and the New York-Northern New Jersey Region. Current Issues in Economics and Finance*, 18, no. 7 (2012).

[16] International Labour Organization, *High Unemployment and Growing Inequality Fuel Social Unrest Around the World*. January 29, 2024.

[17] Jobvite, *The Real Cost of Employee Turnover (and How to Prevent It)*. Jobvite | Recruiting Software - Applicant Tracking (blog), August 14, 2024.

[18] The Manufacturing Institute, *The Case for Second chance Hiring*. 2018.

[19] American Civil Liberties Union, *Human Rights and Criminal Justice*. February 15, 2022.

[20] Fwd.us, *Every Second.* December 2018.

Chapter 2

[1] McCarthy, Patrick, Vincent N. Schiraldi, and Miriam Shark, *The Future of Youth Justice: A Community-Based Alternative to the Youth Prison Model.* 2016.

[2] Clay, Hal, *Forty Acres and a Mule: America's Bill for Reparations Is Long Pas Overdue,* The Scholar: St. Mary's Law Review on Race and Social Justice. 2022.

[3] Foner, Eric, *Reconstruction: America's Unfinished Revolution, 1863-1877. New American Nation Series,* New York: Harper & Row, Publishers, 1988.

[4] Litwack, Leon F., *Been in the Storm So Long: The Aftermath of Slavery.* Vintage, 1980.

[5] Blackmon, Douglas A., *Slavery by Another Name: The Re-Enslavement of Black Americans from the Civil War to World War II.* Anchor, 2009.

[6] Onion, Amanda, *Black Codes - Definition, Dates & Jim Crow Laws. HISTORY,* March 29, 2023.

[7] Prison Policy Initiative, *Race and Ethnicity. Prison Policy Initiative,* 2024.

[8] Nixon, Richard, *Special Message to the Congress on Drug Abuse Prevention and Control. The American Presidency Project,* 1971.

[9] Tonry, Michael, *Malign Neglect: Race, Crime, and Punishment in America.* Oxford University Press, 1995.

[10] Dillingham, Steven D., *Correctional Populations in the United States, 1989.* Washington, DC: U.S. Department of Justice, 1991.

[11] Mauer, Marc, *Race to Incarcerate.* The New Press, 2006.

[12] Congress.gov | Library of Congress, *Text - H.R.3355 - 103rd Congress (1993-1994): Violent Crime Control and Law Enforcement Act of 1994,* 1994.

[13] *New Jim Crow - Mass Incarceration in the Age of Colorblindness, Office of Justice Programs,* 2012.

[14] American Civil Liberties Union, *Report: The War on Marijuana in Black and White. American Civil Liberties Union,* January 19, 2024.

[15] *World Population Review, Incarceration Rates by Country 2024,* 2024.

[16] Prison Policy Initiative, *United States Profile. Prison Policy Initiative,* 2023.

[17] Wessler, Mike, *New Report: Mass Incarceration - The Whole Pie 2023 Shows That as the Pandemic Subsides, Criminal Legal System Returning to 'Business as Usual.' Prison Policy Initiative,* March 14, 2023.

[18] Reaves, Brian A., *Felony Defendants in Large Urban Counties, 2009—Statistical Tables.* Washington, DC: U.S. Department of Justice, 2013.

[19] United States Sentencing Commission, *2023 Annual Report,* July 16, 2024.

[20] U.S. Sentencing Commission, *Quick Facts: Federal Offenders in Prison.* Published January 2024.

[21] Falk, Örjan, Märta Wallinius, Sebastian Lundström, Thomas Frisell, Henrik Anckarsäter, and Nóra Kerekes, *The 1% of the Population Accountable for 63% of All Violent Crime Convictions. Social Psychiatry and Psychiatric Epidemiology,* 49, 2014.

[22] Lopez, German and Javier Zarracina, *Study: Black People Are 7 Times More Likely Than White People to Be Wrongly Convicted of Murder. Vox,* March 7, 2017.

[23] Alper, Mariel, Matthew R. Durose, and Joshua Markman, *2018 Update on Prisoner Recidivism: A 9-Year Follow-Up Period (2005-2014).* Washington, DC: U.S. Department of Justice, Office of Justice Programs, Bureau of Justice Statistics, 2018.

[24] Avery, Beth, Maurice Emsellem, and Phil Hernandez, *Fair Chance Licensing Reform: Opening Pathways for People with Records to Join Licensed Professions.* 2018.

[25] Illinois Policy, *How Occupational Licensing Blocks Path to Success for Ex-Offenders,* April 7, 2015.

[26] Prison Policy Initiative, *Nowhere to Go: Homelessness Among Formerly Incarcerated People.* Prison Policy Initiative, August 2018.

[27] Scott-Clayton, Judith, *Thinking Beyond the Box: The Use of Criminal Records in College Admissions. Brookings,* September 28, 2017.

[28] Center for American Progress, *Federal Financial Aid for College Students With Criminal Convictions,* December 17, 2020.

[29] Prison Policy Initiative, *Prisons of Poverty: Uncovering the Pre-Incarceration Incomes of the Imprisoned.* Prison Policy Initiative, July 9, 2015.

[30] Nam, Jane, *Prison Education Programs: Facts and Statistics. BestColleges.com,* July 11, 2023.

[31] Yen, Rachel, *Does Stable Employment Post-Release Reduce Recidivism? Council on Criminal Justice,* May 30, 2024.

[32] Trone Private Sector and Education Advisory Council to the American Civil Liberties Union, *Back to Business: How Hiring Formerly Incarcerated Job Seekers Benefits Your Company.* New York: ACLU Foundation, 2017.

[33] Televerde, *Televerde's Proven Revenue Growth Model,* November 25, 2024.

[34] Perkins, Eric, *Second chance employment for ex-cons at Dave's Killer Bread.* Cafferty & Scheidegger, 2023.

[35] Earnings Report, *Flowers Reports Fourth Quarter, Full Year 2023 Results.* Flower Foods, December 31, 2023.

Chapter 3

[1] Federal Register, *Annual Determination of Average Cost of Incarceration Fee (COIF).* September 22, 2023.

[2] Vera Institute of Justice, *The Price of Jails.* June 9, 2022.

[3] Hanson, Melanie, *U.S. Public Education Spending Statistics [2024]: Per Pupil + Total.* Education Data Initiative, July 14, 2024.

APPENDIX

[4] Felony Murder Elimination Project, *Cost Per Incarcerated Person in CA Hits Record High*. February 26, 2024.

[5] Hanson, Melanie, *U.S. Public Education Spending Statistics [2024]: Public Education Spending California*. Education Data Initiative, July 14, 2024.

[6] Department of Justice, *Fiscal Year 2024 Funding Request*. March 9, 2023.

[7] Beshay, *Fewer Than 1% of Federal Criminal Defendants Were Acquitted in 2022*. Pew Research Center, April 14, 2024.

[8] The Steep Cost of Capital Punishment. Milken Institute Review, November 13, 2023.

[9] Amnesty International USA, *Death Penalty Cost*. June 26, 2023.

[10] *Capital Punishment or Life Imprisonment? Some Cost Considerations*. Office of Justice Programs, November 1989.

[11] Franicevic, Alan Vinegrad and Zora. *"Federal Pretrial Diversion Programs: Past, Present, and Future."* New York Law Journal, November 30, 2023.

[12] New York Law Journal, *Federal Pretrial Diversion Programs: Past, Present, and Future*. November 2023.

[13] News From The States, *Pretrial Diversion Programs Are Effective. And Expensive for Participants*. March 28, 2024.

[14] RTI, *Study: Replacing Prison Terms With Drug Abuse Treatment Could Save Billions in Criminal Justice Costs*. January 9, 2013.

[15] *Department of Justice (DOJ) | Spending Profile | USAspending*. September 30, 2024.

[16] *BOP: Population Statistics*. January 12, 2025.

[17] Schoenherr, Neil, *Cost of Incarceration in the U.S. More Than $1 Trillion - The Source - Washington University in St. Louis*. The Source, November 24, 2020.

[18] *Gross Domestic Product, Fourth Quarter and Year 2023 (Second Estimate) | U.S. Bureau of Economic Analysis (BEA)*. February 28, 2024.

[19] Fwd.us, *Every Second.* December 2018.

[20] National Institute of Justice, *Hidden Consequences: The Impact of Incarceration on Dependent Children.* 2022.

[21] Admin, *Half of Americans Have Family Members Who Have Been Incarcerated.* Equal Justice Initiative, June 3, 2022.

[22] deVuono-Powell, Saneta, Chris Schweidler, Alicia Walters, and Azadeh Zohrabi, *Who Pays? The True Cost of Incarceration on Families.* Oakland, CA: Ella Baker Center, Forward Together, Research Action Design, 2015.

[23] Clear, Todd R., *The Effects of High Imprisonment Rates on Communities. Crime and Justice* 37, no. 1, 2008.

[24] McGillivray, Candice, *Rendering Them Visible: A Review of Progress Towards Increasing Awareness and Support of Prisoners' Families. Drugs,* 2009.

[25] Annie E. Casey Foundation, *A Shared Sentence: The Devastating Toll of Parental Incarceration on Kids, Families, and Communities. Kids Count Policy Report,* 2016.

[26] Feinstein, Leon, Kathryn Duckworth, and Ricardo Sabates, *Education and the Family: Passing Success Across the Generations.* Routledge, 2008.

[27] Bureau of Justice Assistance, *Justice Reinvestment Initiative (JRI) | Overview.* November 9, 2023.

[28] Bronson , Jennifer and Marcus Berzofsky, *Indicators of Mental Health Problems Reported by Prisoners and Jail Inmates, 2011–12. Bureau of Justice Statistics Special Issue,* 2017.

[29] Karberg, Jennifer C. and Doris J. James, *Substance Dependence, Abuse, and Treatment of Jail Inmates, 2002,* 2005.

[30] Harwood, Henrick J. and Ellen Bouchery, *The Economic Costs of Drug Abuse in the United States, 1992-2002.* Washington, DC, USA: Executive Office of the President, Office of National Drug Control Policy, 2004.

[31] National Drug Intelligence Center, *The Economic Impact of Illicit Drug Use on American Society*. Washington, DC: United States Department of Justice, 2011.

[32] The Council of Economic Advisers, *Returns on Investments in Recidivism-Reducing Programs*. Washington, DC: Executive Office of the President, May 2018.

[33] De Andrade, Dominique, Jessica Ritchie, Michael Rowlands, Emily Mann, and Leanne Hides, *Substance Use and Recidivism Outcomes for Prison-Based Drug and Alcohol Interventions. Epidemiologic Reviews* 40, 2018.

[34] Sarah Knopf-Amelung, *Incarceration & Homelessness: A Revolving Door of Risk. Focus: A Quarterly Research Review of the National HCH Council* 2, 2013.

[35] National Alliance to End Homelessness, *Housing First*. August 2022. Retrieved January 15, 2025.

[36] U.S. Sentencing Commission, *Measuring Recidivism: The Criminal History Computation of the Federal Sentencing Guidelines*. Washington, DC, 2004.

[37] Duwe, Grant and Makada Henry-Nickie, *A Better Path Forward for Criminal Justice: Training and Employment for Correctional Populations*. Brookings, April 30, 2021.

[38] Prison Entrepreneurship Program, *PEP Results: Impact and Scalability*. 2024.

[39] Defy Ventures, *Our Results: Defying the Odds*. 2024.

[40] Justice Through Code, *Our Results: Defying the Odds. Columbia University Center for Justice,* 2024.

[41] RAND, *Education and Vocational Training in Prisons Reduces Recidivism, Improves Job Outlook*. August 22, 2013.

[42] Melhorn, Stephanie Ferguson, Makinizi Hoover, and Isabella Lucy, *The Workforce Impact of Second chance Hiring*. U.S. Chamber of Commerce, September 18, 2024.

Chapter 4

[1] Gurchiek, Kathy, *Research: Employers Willing to Overlook a Criminal Record to Hire the Right Person.* SHRM, December 21, 2023.

[2] Cumming, Ben, *Unlocking the Potential of Justice-Impacted Talent. MIT Sloan Management Review* 64, 2023.

[3] MIT Sloan, *The Bottom-Line Benefits of Second chance Hiring.* July 18, 2024.

[4] Gale, Sarah Fister, *A Second chance: How Nehemiah's Unconventional Hiring Program Is Slashing Turnover and Changing Lives. Chief Learning Officer,* June 17, 2021.

[5] Heinz, Kate, *The True Costs of Employee Turnover.* Built In, July 17, 2024.

[6] McGee, Simeon, *Recruitment Fees: The Cost of Using an Agency in 2023.* EddySoftware, 2024.

[7] Employment Development Department, *Work Opportunity Tax Credit,* 2024.

[8] Department of Labor, *WOTC Program,* 2024.

[9] Cost Management Services Work Opportunity Tax Credits Experts, *Work Opportunity Tax Credit Statistics 2022.* March 9, 2023.

[10] *The Federal Bonding Program: A US Department of Labor Initiative.* National Institute of Corrections, 2013.

[11] Douglas, Roberta "Toni" Meyers, *Federal Bonding Program.* Legal Action Center, April 19, 2024.

[12] Federal Bonding Program, *What Employers Are Saying.* October 5, 2017.

[13] Bhattarai, Abha and Maggie Penman, *Restaurants Can't Find Workers Because They've Found Better Jobs. Washington Post,* February 14, 2023.

[14] NRA, *A New Normal Takes Hold; Restaurants Focused on Paths to Continued Growth in 2023,* 2023.

[15] *Second chances through the Culinary Arts: An Innovative Reentry Partnership. Chopping for Change.* Lutheran Metropolitan Ministry, 2022.

[16] Bureau of Labor Statistics, *Software Developers, Quality Assurance Analysts, and Testers,* August 29, 2024.

[17] The Last Mile, *Home - the Last Mile,* November 9, 2024.

[18] Bureau of Labor Statistics, *Construction Laborers and Helpers,* August 29, 2024.

[19] CEO, *What Does the Increase in Demand for Justice-Impacted Workers Mean?* October 20, 2022.

[20] MIT Sloan, *The Bottom-line Benefits of Second chance Hiring,* July 18, 2024.

[21] *2023 Impact Report: 20th Anniversary Edition.* The Source, 2023.

[22] Gallup, Inc., *How to Improve Employee Engagement in the Workplace.* Gallup.com, November 18, 2024.

[23] Boskamp, Elsie, *60+ Incredible Diversity in the Workplace Statistics [2023]: Facts You Need to Know.* Zippia, June 28, 2023.

[24] Checkr, *Four in Five U.S. Workers Want Employers to Hire People With Conviction Histories [New Checkr Report].* Checkr Blog, July 3, 2024.

[25] *CSR And Profitability: How Doing Good Increases Your Returns,* 2024.

[26] Cone, C., *Cone Communications CSR Study,* 2017.

[27] Murillo, Ruben Hernandez and Christopher J. Martinek, *Corporate Social Responsibility Can Be Profitable,* St. Louis Fed, September 29, 2023.

[28] Milano, Gregory V., Brian Tomlinson, and Riley Whately, *The Return on Purpose: Before and During a Crisis,* SSRN Electronic Journal, January 1, 2020.

[29] Hower, Mike, *50% of Global Consumers Willing to Pay More for Socially Responsible Products,* Sustainable Brands, August 12, 2013.

[30] Witkin, Andrew, *EQ Quotient: Emotional Engagement in Building Brand Loyalty,* Brandingmag, September 4, 2023.

Chapter 5

[1] Davis, Lois M., Robert Bozick, Jennifer L. Steele, Jessica Saunders, and Jeremy N. Miles, *Evaluating the Effectiveness of Correctional Education: A Meta-Analysis of Programs That Provide Education to Incarcerated Adults,* RAND, August 22, 2013.

[2] Duwe, Grant and Makada Henry-Nickie, *A Better Path Forward for Criminal Justice: Training and Employment for Correctional Populations,* Brookings, April 30, 2021.

[3] Burkhardt, Brett C., *Criminal Punishment, Labor Market Outcomes, and Economic Inequality: Devah Pager's: Marked: Race, Crime, and Finding Work in an Era of Mass Incarceration, Law & Social Inquiry* 34, 2009.

[4] The Editors of Encyclopedia Britannica, *Pierre Bourdieu | Biography, Theories, Works, & Facts, Encyclopedia Britannica,* December 12, 2024.

[5] Putnam, Robert D. *Bowling Alone: The Collapse and Revival of American Community.* Paperback ed., Simon & Schuster, 2001.

[6] Ostrom, Brian J., Lydia E. Hamblin, Richard Y. Schauffler, and Nial Raaen. "Timely Justice in Criminal Cases: What the Data Tells Us." *National Center for State Courts,* 2020.

[7] American Bar Association, Judicial Administration Division. *Standards Relating to Appellate Courts.* American Bar Association, 1994.

[8] United States Sentencing Commission. "Individuals in the Federal Bureau of Prisons," September 25, 2024.

[9] Timmer, Anastasiia, Oshea D. Johnson, and Kathryn M. Nowotny. "Multiple Disadvantage and Social Networks: Toward an Integrated Theory of Health Care Use During Reentry From Criminal Justice Settings." *International Journal of Offender Therapy and Comparative Criminology*, 2022.

[10] Urrutia, Cynthia Beatriz. "Ex-Prisoners' Reintegration Into Society: A Look at How Employment Affects Reintegration, 2012.

Chapter 6

[1] Yuki. "Norway's Prison System Benefits Its Economy." *The Borgen Project,* January 6, 2021.

[2] James, Erwin. "The Norwegian Prison Where Inmates Are Treated Like People." *The Guardian,* November 25, 2017.

[3] Pratt, John. "Scandinavian Exceptionalism in an Era of Penal Excess: Part I: The Nature and Roots of Scandinavian Exceptionalism." *The British Journal of Criminology* 48, 2008.

[4] Regeringen och Regeringskansliet. "The Swedish National Council for Crime Prevention." *Regeringskansliet,* 2021.

[5] Denny, Meagan. *Bridges: A Journal of Student Research | Journals and Peer-Reviewed Series | Coastal Carolina University,* 2016.

[6] Johnsen, Berit, Per Kristian Granheim, and Janne Helgesen. "Exceptional Prison Conditions and the Quality of Prison Life: Prison Size and Prison Culture in Norwegian Closed Prisons." *European Journal of Criminology* 8, 2011.

[7] Kriminalvården, Swedish Prison and Probation Service. *Rehabilitation,* 2021.

[8] First Step Alliance. "Rehabilitation Lessons From Norway's Prison System." *First Step Alliance (blog),* May 2, 2024.

[9] World Prison Brief. *Recidivism Rates in Norway,* 2023.

[10] The Swedish National Council for Crime Prevention. *Recidivism in Sweden,* 2021.

[11] BBC News. "How Norway Turns Criminals Into Good Neighbours," July 6, 2019.

[12] Lappi-Seppälä, Tapio. "Explaining Imprisonment in Europe." *European Journal of Criminology* 8, July 1, 2011.

[13] Subramanian, Ram, and Alison Shames. "Sentencing and Prison Practices in Germany and the Netherlands: Implications for the United States." *VERA Institute of Justice,* October 2013. *Federal Sentencing Reporter* 27, 2014.

[14] Stinson, Jill A. "We've Got Some Work to Do: How the United States Could Benefit From Implementing Germany's Prison Employment Program." *Indiana International & Comparative Law Review* 33, 2023

[15] McGuire, Shannon Leigh. *A Cross-National Analysis on the U.S. and German Prison Model.* Bachelor of Science in Criminology and Criminal Justice, 2022.

[16] Fluke. "European Prison Regime Forum Workshop by Europris – EPEA," November 13, 2017.

[17] Fluke. "European Prison Regime Forum Workshop by Europris – EPEA," March 2004.

[18] Brooker, Charlie, and Jorge Monteiro. *Prisons and Probation: A Council of Europe White Paper Regarding the Management of Persons with Mental Health Disorders.* PC-CP (2021) 8 Rev 9. Strasbourg: Council of Europe, September 22, 2022.

[19] Jehle, Jörg-Martin. *Criminal Justice in Germany: Facts and Figures.* Forum-Verlag Godesberg GmbH, 2019.

[20] Recidivism Rate of Male Inmates When Considering Vocational Training, General Education Development Tests, and the Conditions of Release From Prison. *Office of Justice Programs,* 1976.

[21] European Union Agency for Fundamental Rights. "Fundamental Rights Report 2021," November 18, 2024.

[22] Restorative Justice Service Review | New Zealand Ministry of Justice, July 2023.

23 Pfander, Sarah Mikva. "Evaluating New Zealand's Restorative Promise: The Impact of Legislative Design on the Practice of Restorative Justice." *Kōtuitui New Zealand Journal of Social Sciences Online* 15, no. 1 October 27, 2019.

24 Van Camp, Tinneke, and Jo-Anne Wemmers. "Victim Satisfaction with Restorative Justice: More Than Simply Procedural Justice." *International Review of Victimology* 19, no. 2, 2013.

25 MIRI - McMaster Indigenous Research Institute. "Prison Education Project - MIRI - McMaster Indigenous Research Institute," November 6, 2024.

26 Jess. "Bridging the Digital Divide: Navigating the Challenges of Digital Access for Incarcerated (and Formerly Incarcerated) Individuals." *Community Tech Network,* June 20, 2024.

27 Bruyns, H. J., and Cecile Nieuwenhuizen. "The Role of Education in the Rehabilitation of Offenders: Perspectives on Higher Education." *South African Journal of Higher Education* 17, no. 2, 2003.

28 Finnie, Ross, Michael Dubois, and Masashi Miyairi. "Post-Graduation Earnings Outcomes of Ontario Transfer Students: Evidence from PSE-Tax Linked Data." 2021.

29 Miller, Sheridan. "Higher Education Behind Bars: Expanding Post-Secondary Educational Programs in New England Prisons and Jails." *New England Board of Higher Education*, 2021.

30 Correctional Service Canada. "Essential Skills Training." *Canada.ca,* January 2, 2024.

31 Social Exclusion Unit. "Reducing Reoffending by Ex-Prisoners." *Cabinet Office,* 2002.

Chapter 7

[1] SHRM. "New SHRM and CKI Survey Highlights Value of Workers With Criminal Records." *SHRM,* December 12, 2023.

[2] Flake, Dallan F. "When Any Sentence Is a Life Sentence: Employment Discrimination Against Ex-Offenders." *Washington University Law Review* 93, 2015.

[3] National Employment Law Project. "Unlicensed & Untapped: Removing Barriers to State Occupational Licenses for People With Records." *National Employment Law Project,* April 8, 2024.

[4] Davis, Lois M. "Higher Education Programs in Prison: What We Know Now and What We Should Focus on Going Forward." *RAND,* August, 2019.

[5] Avery, Beth, and Han Lu. "Ban The Box: U.S. Cities, Counties, and States Adopt Fair Hiring Policies." *National Employment Law Project,* April 27, 2024.

[6] Leins, Casey. "More Data Needed to Determine Whether 'Ban the Box' Laws Work." *U.S. News & World Report,* September 10, 2019.

[7] "Bill Text - AB-1008 Employment Discrimination: Conviction History." 2018.

[8] Hernandez, Phil. "Ban-the-Box 'Statistical Discrimination' Studies Draw the Wrong Conclusions." *National Employment Law Project,* August 29, 2017.

[9] DOL. "Work Opportunity Tax Credit," 2022.

[10] National Employment Law Project. "Fair Chance Licensing." *National Employment Law Project,* August 29, 2024.

[11] "Benefits After Incarceration: What You Need to Know | Transitioning From Incarceration: Statewide Prerelease Agreements." *SSA,* 2024.

[12] Hager, Eli. "Six States Where Felons Can't Get Food Stamps." *The Marshall Project,* February 4, 2016.

[13] Maurer, Roy. *House Passes Fair Chance Act.* SHRM, December 21, 2023.

[14] Smith, Allen, JD. *Clean Slate Laws Are Spreading.* SHRM, March 25, 2024.

15 Prescott, J.J, and Sonja B. Starr. *Expungement of Criminal Convictions: An Empirical Study*. Harv. L. Rev. 133, no. 8 (2020): 2460-555

16 Reavis, Cate, Daniel Dart, and Blake Blaze. *Checkr and Fair Chance Hiring*. MIT Sloan School of Management. March 29, 2024.

17 Office of Advocacy. *Frequently Asked Questions About Small Business, 2023*. U.S. Small Business Administration. March 7, 2023.

18 Vaught, Grant. *US Department of Labor Awards $725K to Help At-Risk Works Overcome Barriers to Employment*. U.S. Department of Labor. April 2021.

19 Monthly Labor Review. *Professional certifications and occupational licenses: evidence from the Current Population Survey*. U.S. Bureau Of Labor Statistics. June 2019.

20 Castro, Erin, Marc Howard, Laura Ferguson Mimms, and Rachel Zolensky. *Commentary: Improving prison education programs*. The Brookings Institution. February 13, 2024.

21 Research Library. *Research on the prevalence and treatment of mental illness in the criminal legal system*. The Prison Policy Initiative. 2016-2025.

Chapter 8

1 National Employment Law Project. "Faulty FBI Background Checks for Employment: Correcting FBI Records Is Key to Criminal Justice Reform." *National Employment Law Project,* April 8, 2024.

2 Shumway, Emilie. "Background Checks Include 'Lots of Inaccuracies,' Researchers Find." *HR Dive,* February 23, 2024.

3 Why Are Diversity and Inclusion Critical in the Workplace? *Penn LPS Online,* September 28, 2022.

Chapter 9

[1] West, Charlotte. "We Surveyed People in Prison About How They Use Technology. Their Answers Paint a Glitchy Future." *Slate Magazine,* September 28, 2023.

[2] Sung, Yao-Ting, Kuo-En Chang, and Tzu-Chien Liu. "The Effects of Integrating Mobile Devices With Teaching and Learning on Students' Learning Performance: A Meta-analysis and Research Synthesis." *Computers & Education* 94, November 23, 2015

[3] Imber, Dan. "The Latest Tesla Statistics," January 14, 2025.

[4] Stone, Maddie. "EV Batteries Are Dangerous to Repair. Here's Why Mechanics Are Doing so Anyway." *Scientific American,* February 20, 2024.

[5] Vorecol.com. "The Role of Artificial Intelligence in Enhancing Performance Management," 2024.

[6] Kelley, Erin M., Christopher Ksoll, and Jeremy Magruder. How Do Online Job Portals Affect Employment and Job Search? 2022.

[7] Cardoni, Vanessa. Skills-Based Hiring for Justice-impacted Citizens. *Goodwill Industries International,* June 14, 2023.

[8] Devi, R. Sharmila, and Swamy Perumandla. "Revolutionizing Recruitment: Skill-Based Interview Models in the Artificial Intelligence-Driven Economy." In *AI-Oriented Competency Framework for Talent Management in the Digital Economy*, CRC Press. 2024

[9] Romanna. "Virtual Career Fairs: The Ultimate Guide (2025) - vFairs.com." *vFairs.Com* (blog), November 19, 2024.

[10] Matsuda, Norihiko, and Ryotaro Hayashi. "The Impact of an Online Job Fair: Experimental Evidence from Bangladesh. 2024.

[11] Sells, Dave, Anderson Curtis, Jehan Abdur-Raheem, Michele Klimczak, Charles Barber, Cathleen Meaden, Jacob Hasson, Patrick Fallon, and Meredith Emigh-

Guy. "Peer-Mentored Community Reentry Reduces Recidivism." *Criminal Justice and Behavior* 47, 2020.

[12] Randall, Megan, and Katharine Ligon. "From Recidivism to Recovery: The Case for Peer Support in Texas Correctional Facilities." *Center for Public Policy Priorities,* 2019. Retrieved April 15, 2024.

[13] Sainju, Karla Dhungana, Stephanie Fahy, Booz Allen Hamilton, Katherine Baggaley, Ashley Baker, Tamar Minassian, and Vanessa Filippelli. "Electronic Monitoring for Pretrial Release: Assessing the Impact." *Federal Probation* 82, 2018.

[14] U.S. Department of Justice, Office of Justice Programs, National Institute of Justice. *Toward Criminal Justice Solutions.* September 2011.

[15] Council of State Governments Justice Center. *50 States, 1 Goal: Examining State-Level Recidivism Trends in the Second chance Act Era.* April 2024.

ABOUT THE AUTHOR

Nevin Shetty is a seasoned financial executive and strategic leader whose career spans hedge fund management, early stage and growth stage technology companies, corporate turnarounds, and family office operations.

As a CFO, Mr. Shetty has collectively raised over $300M from pension funds, private equity funds and venture capital funds. Shetty's financial acumen and operational leadership has led to the creation of more than $1.5 billion of shareholder value.

Shetty holds a B.A. and a Master's in Professional Accounting from the University of Washington. Mr. Shetty earned his Certified Public Accountant (CPA) designation in 2009 and his Chartered Financial Analyst (CFA) designation in 2011.

For more information about Nevin Shetty and his work, please visit www.nevinshetty.com.

www.ingramcontent.com/pod-product-compliance
Lightning Source LLC
Chambersburg PA
CBHW031108250726

48655CB00004B/1630